The Rise and Fall of World Powers

The Rise and Fall of World Powers

by
John MacArthur, Jr.

MOODY PRESS

CHICAGO

© 1989 by
JOHN F. MACARTHUR, JR.

All Scripture quotations, unless noted otherwise, are from the *New Scofield Reference Bible*, King James Version. Copyright © 1967 by Oxford University Press, Inc. Reprinted by permission.

ISBN: 0-8024-5377-5

1 2 3 4 5 6 7 8 Printing/LC/Year 93 92 91 90 89

Printed in the United States of America

Contents

These Bible studies are taken from messages delivered by Pastor-Teacher John MacArthur, Jr., at Grace Community Church in Panorama City, California. The recorded messages themselves may be purchased as a series or individually. Please request the current price list by writing to:

WORD OF GRACE COMMUNICATIONS
P.O. Box 4000
Panorama City, CA 91412

Or call the following toll-free number:
1-800-55-GRACE

1
Forgotten Dream and the Unforgettable Daniel

Outline

Introduction

Lesson
I. The Forgotten Dream (vv. 1-13)
   A. The Dream (vv. 1-3)
      1. The king's response (v. 1)
      2. The king's request (vv. 2-3)
         a) Gathering the experts
            (1) Magicians
            (2) Astrologers
            (3) Sorcerers
            (4) Chaldeans
         b) Presenting the problem
   B. The Dilemma (vv. 4-9)
      1. The Chaldeans' confidence (v. 4)
      2. The king's challenge (vv. 5-6)
      3. The Chaldeans' claim (v. 7)
      4. The king's cynicism (vv. 8-9)
   C. The Deficiency (vv. 10-11)
      1. Confessed (v. 10)
      2. Contrasted (v. 11)
   D. The Decree (vv. 12-13)
II. The Unforgettable Daniel (vv. 14-30)
   A. His Composure (vv. 14-15)
      1. A calm attitude (v. 14)
      2. A careful question (v. 15)
   B. His Courage (v. 16)

Introduction

George Washington once said, "Few men have virtue to withstand the highest bidder" (*Maxims of Washington*, John Frederick Schroeder, ed. [N.Y.: D. Appleton, 1855], p. 311). He was right. Most people have a price. An uncompromising man or woman is a rare commodity. But that's exactly the kind of person God wants to do His work. He wants choice servants for choice ministries.

Daniel was such a person—he wouldn't compromise (Dan. 1). So God used him to reveal His redemptive plan for Israel and the nations of the world. In Daniel 2 we find the most comprehensive, prophetic picture of human history in the Old Testament. God chose Daniel because his uncompromising virtue and character put him in a position to influence the world through his prophecy.

The first thirty verses of chapter 2 can be divided into two simple thoughts: the forgotten dream (vv. 1-13) and the unforgettable Daniel (vv. 14-30). Daniel received a divine commission to reveal God's plan in the midst of a crisis.

Lesson

I. THE FORGOTTEN DREAM (vv. 1-13)

A. The Dream (vv. 1-3)

1. The king's response (v. 1)

"In the second year of the reign of Nebuchadnezzar, Nebuchadnezzar dreamed dreams, and his spirit was troubled, and his sleep went from him."

In Daniel 2:28-29 Daniel says to King Nebuchadnezzar of Babylon, "Thy dream, and the visions of thy head upon thy bed, are these: As for thee, O king, thy thoughts came into thy mind upon thy bed, what should come to pass hereafter." Lying in his bed one night, Nebuchadnezzar wondered what would happen to the world after he died.

Cataclysmic things had already taken place. The Babylonians had recently supplanted the Assyrian Empire and decisively defeated Egypt, which would never fully rise from its ashes. Israel had been taken captive, and Judah was in the process of dissolution.

Apparently God gave Nebuchadnezzar several dreams, for the Hebrew word translated "dreams" is plural. But I believe one particular dream gave him the most anxiety. The Hebrew word translated "troubled" refers to a deep disturbance. Ordinary dreams can trouble a person, but not with the intensity indicated here. Nebuchadnezzar's dream troubled him because it was God-ordained.

Dreams Ordained to Reveal the Truth

It was not that unusual for God to reveal His plans in dreams to people in the past. Numbers 12:6 says that the Lord spoke to the prophets in visions and dreams. In Genesis 28:10-15 Jacob had a

9

dream that promised him the land of Palestine. God spoke in dreams to Joseph (Gen. 37:5-10), Abimelech (Gen. 20:3), and Solomon (1 Kings 3:5-15). God revealed to Pharaoh in a dream that Egypt would experience seven years of plenty followed by seven years of famine (Gen. 41:1-8). Through a dream God indirectly provided encouragement to Gideon and his men (Judg. 7:13-15). God no longer speaks through dreams because He has completed His revelation. Hebrews 1:2 says He "hath in these last days spoken unto us by his Son." But in former days, God chose to speak through dreams.

Nebuchadnezzar's dream panicked him. To make matters worse he couldn't remember the details. (I believe God removed most of them from his memory.) Since only the fear of the dream remained, the king probably spent the remainder of the night in sleepless anxiety. By morning he was an emotional wreck.

    2. The king's request (vv. 2-3)

> "Then the king commanded to summon the magicians, and the astrologers, and the sorcerers, and the Chaldeans, to show the king his dreams. So they came and stood before the king. And the king said unto them, I have dreamed a dream, and my spirit was troubled to know the dream."

    a) Gathering the experts

Nebuchadnezzar appealed to the brain trust of the Babylonian Empire to help him figure out his dream.

(1) Magicians—The Hebrew term translated "magicians" refers to fortune-tellers. It can also refer to scholars. In ancient societies it wasn't unusual to see the two roles combined.

(2) Astrologers—These stargazers charted the positions of the stars and, on the basis of how they were arranged, tried to determine peoples' destinies, much like those who make up horoscopes claim to do today.

(3) Sorcerers—These spiritualists and enchanters were mediums who attempted to talk with the dead.

(4) Chaldeans—Originally from southern Babylonia, the Chaldeans eventually rose to a place of prominence in the courts of Babylon after Nabopolassar, Nebuchadnezzar's father, himself a Chaldean, became king. Supposedly they were the wisest and most knowledgeable in the arts and sciences of Chaldea (Babylon).

As so many people do today, the king sought out the so-called experts. The king's advisers believed in the importance of dreams, so they were anxious to help the king.

The Chaldean Dream-Reading System

The Chaldean "experts in dreams worked on the principle that dreams and their sequel followed an empirical law which, given sufficient data, could be established. . . . Dream manuals, of which several examples have come to light [see A.L. Oppenheim, "The Interpretation of Dreams in the Ancient Near East," *Transactions of the American Philosophical Society* 46.3 (1956): 203ff.], consist accordingly of historical dreams and the events that followed them, arranged systematically for easy reference. Since these books had to try to cover every possible eventuality they became inordinately long; only the expert could find his way through them, and even he had to know the dream to begin with before he could search for the nearest possible parallel" (Joyce G. Baldwin, *Daniel: An Introduction and Commentary* [Downers Grove, Ill.: Inter-Varsity, 1978], pp. 86-87).

b) Presenting the problem

The king presented a challenging problem for his advisers: he had had a dream, but had forgotten it (v. 3). The king's problem was about to become his advisers' problem.

11

B. The Dilemma (vv. 4-9)

1. The Chaldeans' confidence (v. 4)

"Then spoke the Chaldeans to the king in Aramaic, O king, live forever; tell thy servants the dream, and we will show the interpretation."

This verse begins a lengthy section written in Aramaic instead of Hebrew (Dan. 2:4–7:28). Aramaic was the main language used in the courts, and later in all southwest Asia. The wise men began, "O king, live forever" which is to say, "Long live the king." That phrase was standard court etiquette. Then, with great confidence, they asked the king to recount his dream so that they could interpret it for him. But the king couldn't do so.

2. The king's challenge (vv. 5-6)

"The king answered and said to the Chaldeans, The thing is gone from me. If ye will not make known unto me the dream, with the interpretation of it, ye shall be cut in pieces, and your houses shall be made a refuse heap [dung hill]. But if ye show the dream, and its interpretation, ye shall receive from me gifts and rewards and great honor; therefore, show me the dream, and the interpretation of it."

Nebuchadnezzar put his advisers on the spot. If they couldn't reveal and interpret his dream, they faced ruin. But if they were successful, they would receive great reward and honor.

I believe Nebuchadnezzar was cynical concerning his advisers' system of interpreting dreams. He may have believed the lot of them were nothing more than charlatans. So he put his court wise men to the test to determine if they had been telling the truth in the past and if they were worth his confidence in the future. And he had to know, because forgetting a dream was considered an ominous sign in the Orient: it meant the gods were angry.

12

Commentators translate the phrase "the thing is gone from me" (v. 5) differently. Some believe the king said, "I am sure of it," implying he did know the dream but was holding it back from his advisers. However, I believe he had forgotten the dream—that is the only solution that makes sense to me, given the context. I believe God wanted the king to forget the dream to expose the impotence and deception of Babylonian wisdom. At the same time the king's forgetting the dream established Daniel as the mouthpiece of God unequaled by any of the Babylonian wise men. As the king gave his wise men the ultimate test to determine their integrity and true abilities, he appeared to be tyrannical and unreasonable. Commentator H. C. Leupold has said, "We venture to say that, if the Chaldeans had not made pretense of having access to the deepest and most completely hidden things, the king would never have made this unreasonable request of them" (*Exposition of Daniel* [Grand Rapids: Baker, 1969], p. 89).

The king promised a devastating punishment if he discovered his advisers couldn't interpret his dream: he would cut them to pieces and turn their houses into manure piles. Such a punishment was not uncommon in ancient Middle Eastern cultures when someone had severely dishonored himself or defamed an exalted person. The victim was executed and his house torn down and replaced by a public outhouse (e.g., 2 Kings 10:27). But if the Chaldeans did what the king asked, they were to be greatly rewarded.

3. The Chaldeans' claim (v. 7)

"They answered again and said, Let the king tell his servants the dream, and we will show the interpretation of it."

Not having any other choice, the wise men held their ground. They realized they faced a serious dilemma. They knew they couldn't recount the dream—they didn't have access to divine truth; they couldn't ascend to the supernatural realm. Their pretentious claims would be exposed unless they knew the dream.

4. The king's cynicism (vv. 8-9)

"The king answered and said, I know of certainty that
ye would gain the time, because ye see the thing is gone
from me. But if ye will not make known unto me the
dream, there is but one decree for you; for ye have prepared lying and corrupt words to speak before me, till
the time is changed; therefore tell me the dream, and I
shall know that ye can show me its interpretation."

The king could see that his advisers were stalling. He
knew they had prepared wicked lies for him. That gives
us a true indication of how he felt about his advisers. He
saw the phoniness of their system. He probably remembered past predictions that had never come to pass. He
was cynical about the whole system.

C. The Deficiency (vv. 10-11)

1. Confessed (v. 10)

"The Chaldeans answered before the king, and said,
There is not a man upon the earth that can reveal the
king's matter; therefore, there is no king, lord, nor ruler
that asked such things of any magician, or astrologer, or
Chaldean."

The wise men claimed the king was asking them to do
the impossible. No one can predict the future. Horoscopes aren't reliable apart from demonic influence and
mind control. The only place anyone can read about the
future is in the Bible. The wise men concluded that no
ruler, no matter how great and powerful he might be,
was justified in asking anything like what Nebuchadnezzar was asking.

2. Contrasted (v. 11)

"It is a rare thing that the king requireth, and there is no
other that can reveal it before the king, except the gods,
whose dwelling is not with flesh."

The wise men correctly identified the supernatural as the only source from which such information was available. They were trapped in their inability to gain access to that realm.

D. The Decree (vv. 12-13)

"For this cause the king was angry and very furious, and commanded to destroy all the wise men of Babylon. And the decree went forth that the wise men should be slain; and they sought Daniel and his fellows to be slain."

The wrath of a demanding monarch knows no limitations. The king was angry for several reasons: he couldn't remember the details of a dream that had caused him great fear; he couldn't trust his wise men to tell him the truth; he was convinced they had lied to him in the past; and they criticized him, claiming he had no right to demand of them what he had. So he stooped to the depths some dictators will when their desires are crossed: he ordered that they all be executed.

Daniel and his fellows were sought because they were part of the corps of court advisers. Since they were only apprentices, however, I don't believe they were in the group of wise men who had been summoned by the king.

II. THE UNFORGETTABLE DANIEL (vv. 14-30)

The king's wise men had been forced to admit that only a supernatural being could reveal the details of a forgotten dream to anyone. That admission set the scene for Daniel exactly as God had planned. Daniel was God's man commissioned to reveal prophetic truth at a time of crisis.

Certain character qualities make a person useful to God at such a time. Many people are useful to God when life is calm, but when a crisis hits, those with true commitment are separated from the marginal. Daniel was faced with an angry monarch about to slaughter all his wise men, himself included.

A. His Composure (vv. 14-15)

1. A calm attitude (v. 14)

"Then Daniel answered with counsel and wisdom to Arioch, the captain of the king's guard, who was gone forth to slay the wise men of Babylon."

Daniel was calm and composed even though his life was on the line. He never panicked because he had confidence in God. He knew his destiny rested in God's sovereign will. People who respond like that in a crisis are prepared before the crisis ever comes.

The phrase translated "counsel and wisdom" could easily be translated "wisdom and discretion." Daniel spoke appropriately and reasonably. When the king's guard approached Daniel to inform him of the decree and seize him, Daniel responded appropriately with great counsel, wisdom, and discretion to Arioch, the captain of the guard.

Since the Aramaic root translated "captain" comes from a verb that means "to slay," Arioch may have served as the king's executioner. Although other soldiers in the guard were collecting the various wise men, the captain himself went to see Daniel. That enabled Daniel to have direct access to the king through the king's own executioner.

2. A careful question (v. 15)

"He answered and said to Arioch, the king's captain, Why is the decree so hasty from the king? Then Arioch made the thing known to Daniel."

We can see that God controlled Arioch's response since he took the time to explain the situation. Daniel had the ability in the midst of panic to put people at ease. Daniel was fearless because his life was in God's hands. A man without composure will never have an effective long-range ministry, because ministry involves meeting one crisis after another.

B. His Courage (v. 16)

"Then Daniel went in, and desired of the king that he would give him time, and that he would show the king the [dream and its] interpretation."

Instead of executing Daniel, Arioch apparently arranged an audience with the king for him. Though only a youthful apprentice, Daniel boldly asked the king to give him time to show the king the whole interpretation. Daniel was not at all presumptuous in his request to the king. He knew God had given him the ability to reveal dreams and visions (Dan. 1:17).

The king did not grant the wise men the time they so desperately needed, yet he did grant Daniel an audience. Why? Perhaps he remembered when he first examined Daniel and his friends and found them ten times wiser than the wisest men in Babylon (1:20). But also Daniel was courageous. It's hard not to admire a man with strong confidence in God and the willingness to face a frustrated, raging king.

If you don't have composure and courage, you'll never make it through a crisis. But you can be composed and courageous any time when you know you stand on the authority of God's revealed Word.

C. His Prayer (vv. 17-19a)

1. The request (vv. 17-18)

"Then Daniel went to his house, and made the thing known to Hananiah, Mishael and Azariah, his companions; that they would desire mercies of the God of heaven concerning this secret; that Daniel and his fellows should not perish with the rest of the wise men of Babylon."

Daniel went back to tell his friends that he had been granted time to determine the dream and its interpretation. At once they began to "desire mercies of the God of heaven." That's a long way of saying that they began to pray. Daniel's confidence was in God, so he immediately sought communion with the Lord. God's special servants are people of prayer. Daniel could have depended on his righteous character and his gift of interpreting dreams and visions, but he depended on God. He didn't expect to receive what he needed without prayer. He depended on God's mercy. He didn't look to men's wisdom or in dream books; he got on his knees. God's man in a crisis doesn't take his troubles to other people; he takes them to God. He may ask other people to pray with him as Daniel did, but he knows that God is the source of help.

2. The answer (v. 19a)

"Then was the secret revealed unto Daniel in a night vision."

In the middle of that night of prayer, God revealed His secret to Daniel.

D. His Praise (vv. 19b-23)

1. He blessed God (vv. 19b-22)

"Then Daniel blessed the God of heaven. Daniel answered and said, Blessed be the name of God forever and ever; for wisdom and might are his, and he changeth the times and the seasons; he removeth kings, and setteth up kings; he giveth wisdom unto the wise, and knowledge to those who know understanding; he revealeth the deep and secret things; he knoweth what is in the darkness, and the light dwelleth with him."

Daniel blessed God in what amounts to a hymn of praise. His blessing was directed to "the name of God," which is all that God is. He blessed God for His attributes, such as His wisdom, power, and omniscience.

2. He thanked God (v. 23)

"I thank thee, and praise thee, O thou God of my fathers, who hast given me wisdom and might, and hast

18

made known unto me now what we desired of thee; for thou hast now made known unto us the king's matter."

Daniel thanked God for His blessings and especially for answering his and his friends' urgent prayer request.

E. His Compassion (vv. 24-26)

1. Daniel's plea (v. 24)

"Therefore, Daniel went in unto Arioch, whom the king had ordained to destroy the wise men of Babylon; he went and said thus unto him, Destroy not the wise men of Babylon. Bring me in before the king, and I will reveal unto the king the interpretation."

Daniel went to Arioch to make sure the executioner didn't carry out his assignment. Here we see Daniel, a Hebrew captive, countermanding an order given by the king! I think Daniel was motivated by compassion for the wise men. He knew they were lost in their idolatry and doomed to hell. He didn't want them to die.

2. Arioch's declaration (v. 25)

"Then Arioch brought in Daniel before the king in haste, and said thus unto him, I have found a man of the captives of Judah, that will make known unto the king the interpretation."

With much excitement, Arioch brought Daniel before the king, taking more credit than he deserved. Actually Daniel had approached him, but when you're a servant of the king there's a tendency to do all you can to impress your master.

3. Nebuchadnezzar's question (v. 26)

"The king answered and said to Daniel, whose name was Belteshazzar, Art thou able to make known unto me the dream which I have seen, and the interpretation of it?"

The king put Daniel on the spot. If Daniel couldn't fulfill his claim, there would be an even greater reason for his execution, since he had postponed the carrying out of the king's original command. So he pressed Daniel for a confirmation of his ability.

F. His Humility (vv. 27-30)

In spite of all his gifts, brilliance, and spiritual maturity, Daniel remained humble. He had received extensive training, was ten times wiser than the other wise men, and could interpret visions and dreams. If anyone had anything to be proud of, Daniel did. But he remained humble.

1. The ineffectiveness of the wise men (v. 27)

"Daniel answered in the presence of the king, and said, The secret which the king hath demanded cannot the wise men, the astrologers, the magicians, the soothsayers, reveal unto the king."

Daniel wanted to affirm the futility of astrology and the like. He set the true God against useless dream manuals.

2. The supremacy of God (vv. 28-29)

"But there is a God in heaven who revealeth secrets, and maketh known to the king, Nebuchadnezzar, what shall be in the latter days. Thy dream, and the visions of thy head upon thy bed are these: As for thee, O king, thy thoughts came into thy mind upon thy bed, what should come to pass hereafter; and he who revealeth secrets maketh known to thee what shall come to pass."

God had given the king a dream about the "latter days," which refers to the final portion of a time period. In this case Daniel was referring to the time of the Gentiles, extending to the millennial kingdom.

3. The attitude of Daniel (v. 30)

"But as for me, this secret is not revealed to me for any wisdom that I have more than any living, but for their sakes that shall make known the interpretation to the king, and that thou mightest know the thoughts of thy heart."

Daniel wouldn't take any credit for knowing the king's dream. God is the revealer of secrets. Daniel knew he had been used by God for His purposes.

Conclusion

Daniel was a man for a time of crisis. He was composed and courageous. His relationship to God was strong, as seen by his communion with Him in prayer. And he had the right attitude toward others, revealed by his compassion and humility. Daniel was a rare man, and that's why God used him the way He did. He was a choice servant.

Focusing on the Facts

1. What did George Washington mean when he said, "Few men have virtue to withstand the highest bidder" (see p. 8)?
2. What virtue of Daniel put him in a position to be greatly used of God (see p. 8)?
3. What was the king's response to the dream that he received from God (Dan. 2:1; see p. 9)?
4. When was it normal for God to reveal truth in dreams? Why would it be abnormal today (see pp. 9-10)?
5. What action did the king initially take to find answers to his dream (Dan. 2:2-3; see p. 10)?
6. What did the king's advisers believe about dreams? What tools did they use in their analyses (see p. 11)?
7. Why did the king decide to put his court wise men to the test (see p. 12)?
8. Why didn't God allow Nebuchadnezzar to remember his dream (see p. 13)?
9. According to Daniel 2:8-9, what was the king's analysis of his advisers and their dream-reading system (see p. 14)?
10. What is the only source that can accurately predict the future (Dan. 2:11; see pp. 14-15)?
11. Explain why the king wanted to destroy the wise men of Babylon (Dan. 2:11-12; see p. 15).

12. Why didn't Daniel panic under the threat of death (see p. 16)?
13. What was significant about Arioch's coming to arrest Daniel (see p. 16)?
14. What did the king grant to Daniel that he refused to give to the wise men (see p. 17)?
15. What gave Daniel boldness to go before Nebuchadnezzar (see p. 17)?
16. What did Daniel and his friends do with the time they'd been given to determine the dream and its interpretation (Dan. 2:17-18; see pp. 17-18)?
17. What do we learn about God from Daniel's prayer (Dan. 2:19-23; see pp. 18-19)?
18. How did Daniel reveal his compassion (Dan. 2:24; see p. 19)?
19. Why might Daniel have had reason to be proud? How did he demonstrate his humility (Dan. 2:30; see pp. 20-21)?

Pondering the Principles

1. Do you personally know people who consult mediums and horoscopes to gain direction for their lives? Have you offered them the Word of God as the most trustworthy guide for living? Make a brief study of the following passages to learn what you might share with them to help lead them away from their dependence on the occult to faith in God:

   - occultic practices condemned by God (Ex. 22:18; Lev. 19:26, 31; 20:6; Deut. 18:10-12; Gal. 5:19-21; Rev. 22:15)

   - the tendency of the occult to overshadow divine truth and authority (1 Sam. 15:23; Isa. 8:19-20)

   - demonic influences behind the occult (Acts 16:16-18)

   - the impotence of occultic practices before God (Isa. 44:24-25; Acts 16:18)

   - the association of the occult with false prophets (Jer. 27:9-10)

   - the consequences of occultic practices (1 Chron. 10:13-14; 2 Chron. 33:6, 9-11)

Use these passages to direct your friends toward faith in God: Deuteronomy 29:29; Isaiah 46:9-10; 55:6-8; John 8:12; 16:13.

2. How does your character hold up under crisis? What was the last crisis you faced? How long did it take before you prayed to the Lord for guidance and strength? Do you believe you were fully trusting God for the outcome? Are you spiritually prepared for the next crisis? How do you feel you can best prepare yourself for it? Meditate on the following to increase your confidence in the Lord's protection and deliverance: Psalms 4, 23, 27, and 34.

2
The Rise and Fall of the World—Part 1

Outline

Introduction
A. The Downfall of Governments
B. The Dominion of the Gentiles
   1. Its duration
   2. Its backdrop

Lesson
 I. The Dream Received (vv. 1-30)
   A. The Consummation of History
   B. The Succession of History
II. The Dream Recalled (vv. 31-35)
   A. The Description of the Statue (vv. 31-33)
      1. Its general appearance (v. 31)
         a) Massive
         b) Brilliant
         c) Awesome
      2. Its specific elements (vv. 32-33)
         a) Deteriorating worth
         b) Decreasing weights
   B. The Destruction of the Statue (vv. 34-35)
III. The Dream Revealed (vv. 36-45)
   A. Babylon (vv. 37-38)
      1. Its rule
         a) Romans 13:1
         b) Acts 17:26
      2. Its realm
   B. Medo-Persia (v. 39*a*)
      1. Its succession
      2. Its silver

C. Greece (v. 39*b*)
1. Its apportionment
2. Its army
3. Its authority
D. Rome (vv. 40-43)
1. Reviewed from the past (v. 40)
   a) Its duration (v. 40*a*)
   b) Its destructiveness (v. 40*b*)
2. Revived in the future

Conclusion

Introduction

A. The Downfall of Governments

The eventual decline of the United States isn't something that should shock us. All nations go the way of all flesh, ending in collapse and ruin. Anything established on the wisdom and power of man will suffer the same kind of deterioration man himself has suffered since the Fall. Dissipation is man's history—man is not ascending; he is descending. History reveals a succession of defeats. Empires begin, reach a peak, fade, and then die as others are built out of their ashes. America is deteriorating just as every other nation has in the past. Our nation has feet of clay, like the image in Nebuchadnezzar's dream (Dan. 2:33).

B. The Dominion of the Gentiles

The world is a vast stage with the curtain still down. The actors are behind the curtain preparing for the last scene in the drama of human history. That final scene, the return of the Lord Jesus Christ, will take place in the latter days. The book of Daniel takes us behind that curtain before it rises and gives us insight into the unfolding of the last act of human history.

1. Its duration

Daniel 2:31-45 presents the history of the world under Gentile rule. Jesus said this about it: "Jerusalem shall be

26

trodden down by the Gentiles, until the times of the Gentiles be fulfilled" (Luke 21:24). Those times began with the Babylonian Captivity and will end with the second coming of Christ. We are living in that time period right now. Israel does not possess the fullness of its inheritance as promised in the Abrahamic and Palestinian Covenants (Gen. 15:18; Deut. 30:1-9). Nor does it dwell in peace. Gentile nations have dominated that part of the world since Nebuchadnezzar and will continue to do so to some degree until Jesus comes again.

Daniel 2 reveals how God transferred the leadership of the earth from the Jewish nation to the Gentiles. Israel was to be God's messenger to the world, but Israel tragically failed and will not return to its former glory until Jesus returns.

2. Its backdrop

As we come to the book of Daniel, Israel has been taken into captivity. Daniel himself is a captive, but because of his unique capabilities, he has been elevated to serve in the court of King Nebuchadnezzar as an assistant in Jewish affairs. It is in that important position that he receives the prophecy of Gentile domination through the dream of Nebuchadnezzar.

Comfort for the Israelites

Why did God give a prophecy about Gentile domination at the very time that the domination began? Because the nation of Judah had recently been taken into captivity by Gentiles and God wanted the people to know it wouldn't be a permanent situation. If the Israelites came to believe there was no hope for them as a nation, they would have questioned God's credibility. He had said He would maintain His people and would always keep His covenant with them (2 Sam. 7:16). And He has!

At the time the prophecy was given, Jerusalem was in ruins and the Temple had been torn down. Its sacred vessels had been carried off and placed in the temple of an idol. God's glory had departed from the people (Ezek. 11:22-23). The children of Israel stood weeping

27

on the banks of Babylon without a song in their hearts (Ps. 137:1-4). In this saddened state they wanted to know if God had forsaken them forever and forgotten His covenant. The prophecy of Daniel 2 gives a resounding no.

Before we look at God's revelation through the dream, we need to review Daniel 2:1-30.

Lesson

I. THE DREAM RECEIVED (vv. 1-30)

Nebuchadnezzar, a pagan king who didn't believe in the God of Israel, was lying on his bed one night trying to sleep when he began to think about what would happen to his empire when he died (v. 29). Aware that other empires had come and gone, he fell asleep and dreamed a special dream given him by God: a panorama of history from his reign until the return of Jesus Christ. That's "the times of the Gentiles" Jesus referred to (Luke 21:24).

A. The Consummation of History

Daniel 2:28 frames the dream: "There is a God in heaven who revealeth secrets, and maketh known to the king, Nebuchadnezzar, what shall be in the latter days." The key phrase, "the latter days," is not restricted to Nebuchadnezzar's lifetime. It is an eschatological term in Old Testament prophetical writings referring to God's future dealings with mankind, consummated in the kingdom of Messiah (e.g., Gen. 49:1; Num. 24:14; Deut. 4:30; 31:29; Jer. 23:20; 30:24; 48:47; 49:39; Ezek. 38:16; Dan. 10:14; Hos. 3:5; Mic. 4:1). The Greek term translated "the last days" is used the same way in the New Testament (e.g., Acts 2:17-21; 2 Pet. 3:3-4).

B. The Succession of History

In verses 28-29 Daniel says, "Thy dream, and the visions of thy head upon thy bed are these: As for thee, O king, thy thoughts came into thy mind upon thy bed, *what should come to pass* hereafter; and he who revealeth secrets maketh known to thee *what shall come to pass*" (emphasis added). "What shall come to pass" indicates that Nebuchadnezzar was to learn about a succession of events in history leading to the latter days.

We have seen that although Nebuchadnezzar had the dream, he forgot it (see pp. 9-15). God allowed him to forget it to expose the wise men as phonies and give Daniel an opportunity to answer the king's request. Daniel became the channel of God's revelation.

II. THE DREAM RECALLED (vv. 31-35)

Since the king had forgotten his dream, Daniel had to recount it before he could interpret it: "Thou, O king, sawest, and behold a great image [statue]. This great image, whose brightness was excellent, stood before thee, and the form of it was terrible. This image's head was of fine gold, its breast and its arms of silver, its belly and its thighs of bronze, its legs of iron, its feet part of iron and part of clay. Thou sawest until a stone was cut out without hands, which smote the image upon its feet that were of iron and clay, and broke them to pieces. Then were the iron, the clay, the bronze, the silver, and the gold, broken to pieces together, and became like the chaff of the summer threshing floors; and the wind carried them away, that no place was found for them; and the stone that smote the image became a great mountain, and filled the whole earth."

A. The Description of the Statue (vv. 31-33)

Daniel saw a shining metal statue in human form.

1. Its general appearance (v. 31)

   a) Massive

   The Aramaic term translated "great image" means "immense" or "massive."

   b) Brilliant

   That its "brightness was excellent" tells us the metal in it shone brilliantly.

29

c) Awesome

This statue was "terrible"—it inspired fear. We would say it was awesome. It was so immense that the king was scared to death. Even though he couldn't remember his dream, he could remember that it frightened him.

2. Its specific elements (vv. 32-33)

a) Deteriorating worth

The statue was made of different elements. It started with gold at the top and deteriorated in value to iron and clay at the bottom. The clay (Aram., *hasap*, "baked clay") was most likely a brittle, ceramic tile.

b) Decreasing weights

There also is a corresponding lower specific gravity for each element: gold is heavier than silver, silver is heavier than brass, brass is heavier than iron, and iron is heavier than iron and clay combined. The specific gravities of those metals are 19, 11, 8.5, and 7.8 respectively. The gold caused the top of the statue to be more than twice as heavy as the bottom—the statue was top-heavy. From the brittleness of the bottom of the statue, we learn that the Gentile world is balanced precariously and in a constant process of deterioration until the return of Christ, when it will be smashed and blown away like dust in the wind.

B. The Destruction of the Statue (vv. 34-35)

Daniel 2:34-35 says, "A stone was cut out without hands [it had no human source], which smote the image upon its feet that were of iron and clay, and broke them to pieces. Then were the iron, the clay, the bronze, the silver, and the gold, broken to pieces together, and became like the chaff of the summer threshing floors; and the wind carried them away, that no place was found for them; and the stone that smote the image became a great mountain, and filled the whole earth." The stone takes over the world as the top-heavy image is toppled by a crushing blow at its feet. In rapid succession the image disintegrates, and all its dust is blown away.

III. THE DREAM REVEALED (vv. 36-45)

Having recalled the dream, Daniel proceeded to interpret it: "This is the dream, and we will tell its interpretation before the king" (v. 36). Nebuchadnezzar did not agree or disagree with Daniel in the recounting of his dream. I think he was left speechless—he knew Daniel was accurate, which is why he promoted Daniel to prime minister of Babylon (v. 48).

Daniel didn't interpret the king's dream single-handedly, as verse 36 confirms: "*We* will tell its interpretation" (emphasis added). Some claim that "we" refers to Daniel and his three friends, others to Daniel and God. I think it refers to both God and to Daniel's three friends—they were all involved.

In the interpretation of the dream, Daniel identified four kingdoms: "Thou, O king, art a king of kings; for the God of heaven hath given thee a kingdom, power, and strength, and glory. And wherever the children of men dwell, the beasts of the field and the fowls of the heavens hath he given into thine hand, and hath made thee ruler over them all. Thou art this head of gold. And after thee shall arise another kingdom inferior to thee, and another third kingdom of bronze, which shall bear rule over all the earth. And the fourth kingdom shall be strong as iron, forasmuch as iron breaketh in pieces and subdueth all things; and, as iron that breaketh all these, it shall break in pieces and bruise. And whereas thou sawest the feet and toes, part of potters' clay and part of iron, the kingdom shall be divided; but there shall be in it of the strength of the iron, forasmuch as thou sawest the iron mixed with the miry clay. And as the toes of the feet were part of iron and part of clay, so the kingdom shall be partly strong and partly broken. And whereas thou sawest iron mixed with miry clay, they shall mingle themselves with the seed of men; but they shall not adhere one to another, even as iron is not mixed with clay" (vv. 37-43).

The image represents four world empires in succeeding stages from Nebuchadnezzar to Jesus Christ.

A. Babylon (vv. 37-38)

"Thou, O king, art a king of kings; for the God of heaven hath given thee a kingdom, power, and strength, and glory. And wherever the children of men dwell, the beasts of the field and the fowls of the heavens hath he given into thine hand, and hath made thee ruler over them all. Thou art this head of gold."

1. Its rule

Nebuchadnezzar is addressed in verse 37 as "a king of kings"—a title given him by God, who also had given him "a kingdom, power, and strength, and glory." The New Testament confirms that God establishes governments.

a) Romans 13:1—"There is no power but of God; the powers that be are ordained of God."

b) Acts 17:26—God has "determined the times before appointed, and the bounds of their [the nations'] habitation."

God established Nebuchadnezzar as a supreme monarch. Ezekiel also referred to him as "a king of kings" (Ezek. 26:7). Although Nebuchadnezzar reigned for forty-three years, his kingdom lasted about seventy years. That was also the duration of God's chastening of Israel in the Babylonian Captivity before He allowed the people to return to their land (Jer. 27:6-8; 2 Chron. 36:20-21). God raised up Nebuchadnezzar as His chastening agent. Once Israel's chastening was complete, Nebuchadnezzar's kingdom passed out of existence (Jer. 25:12).

2. Its realm

Nebuchadnezzar's kingdom spread over the most civilized portion of the world in his day—from Egypt and Israel to the Persian Gulf. The statement that his realm encompassed the beasts and the birds (v. 38) is simply a hyperbole to show the extent of his authority. Nebuchadnezzar went beyond the leaders of his time in power and authority. Of the four world empires, no monarch is mentioned after him, only kingdoms. His was the only absolute monarchy; the remaining parts of the image indicate a change in the way rule was rendered. Commentator Leon Wood has said, "Nebuchadnezzar was uniquely responsible for [Babylon's] attaining and maintaining empire status. After him, its power diminished rapidly. It was far more his kingdom than he was its king. The same was not true of any ruler of the succeeding empires" (*A Commentary on Daniel* [Grand Rapids: Zondervan, 1973], p. 67).

Daniel identified Nebuchadnezzar as a "head of gold" (v. 38). Gold was a highly valued metal in the Babylonian Empire. The ancient historian Herodotus visited Babylon about seventy years after the empire fell yet still was able to report that he never had seen such proliferation of gold as what he saw in Babylon. He described temple idols, vessels, and other accoutrements made of "more than twenty-two tons of gold" (*The Histories* 1:180-85).

B. Medo-Persia (v. 39*a*)

"And after thee shall arise another kingdom inferior to thee."

According to verse 32, the second kingdom was represented by the statue's chest and arms of silver, an implication that this kingdom wouldn't have the solidarity of the head. It was a two-fold division instead. That can refer only to the Medo-Persian Empire, made up of the Median and Persian peoples, which supplanted the Babylonian Empire.

1. Its succession

The Aramaic word translated "inferior" literally means "lower." Rather than referring to the second kingdom as inferior qualitatively, I think Daniel was saying that the chest and the arms were lower on the statue, meaning that the kingdom of silver would follow the one of gold. It's not a commentary on the quality or size of the kingdom because the last three empires were progressively larger than the previous ones: Medo-Persia was larger than Babylon, Greece was larger than Medo-Persia, and Rome was larger than Greece. And each was stronger than the one before.

Note that verse 39 refers to the second kingdom without saying anything about it. Of the four kingdoms, this is the only one Daniel said nothing about. Whereas the third kingdom would "bear rule over all the earth," no specifics are given concerning the second one. I believe Daniel's reason was to alleviate Nebuchadnezzar's concern about what kingdom would topple his empire.

2. Its silver

One characteristic of the Medo-Persian Empire was its use of silver, or money. The Medo-Persian Empire developed a vast system of taxation that required taxes to be paid in silver (Herodotus, *The Histories* 3:90-97). Xerxes I, who inherited an incredible fortune from his father, Darius I, as well as from other Persian kings, used it to finance the massive Persian Wars against the Greeks.

Following the Babylonian Empire, the Medo-Persian Empire was established in 538 B.C. under Cyrus the Great. It lasted about two hundred years, until 330 B.C.

C. Greece (v. 39*b*)

"Another third kingdom of bronze, which shall bear rule over all the earth."

Verse 32 says this kingdom was represented by the statue's belly and thighs of bronze. Following the Medo-Persian Empire came the Greek Empire under Alexander the Great, who initially received power and authority from his father, Philip of Macedon.

1. Its apportionment

After Alexander died, the empire was divided among his four generals, but ultimately it had a twofold division between the Seleucids in Syria and the Ptolemies in Egypt.

2. Its army

Daniel characterized the Greek kingdom as bronze, apparently because of its army. Commentator W. A. Criswell said, "It is easy to imagine what an astonishing impression the Greeks must have made on the civilized world. Consider the contrast between their soldiers and the soldiers of the Persian Army. Had you seen a soldier of Media or of Persia in the days when they controlled the civilized world, he would have looked like this: On his head would have been a soft, turban-like covering. He would have been clothed with a tunic with sleeves and with trousers full and long. That would have been the Medo-Persian soldier. But when you saw a Greek soldier he would have had on his head a helmet of brass and on his body a breastplate of brass and before him he would be carrying a shield of brass and a sword of brass. That is why the classic writers of ancient days will refer to the 'brazen coated Greeks.' Brass became a sign and a symbol of Greek conquest and of the Greek empire" (*Expository Sermons on the Book of Daniel* [Grand Rapids: Zondervan, 1976], p. 64). Gold represented Babylon because Babylon was preoccupied with gold. Silver represented Medo-Persia because the Medes and Persians were preoccupied with silver. And brass represented the Greeks because it symbolized the forces of Alexander the Great.

3. Its authority

Verse 39 says that the third kingdom would "bear rule over all the earth." Indeed, Alexander the Great conquered Egypt, part of Europe, and most of the land from Asia Minor to India—practically the entire known world—before he died in his thirties.

D. Rome (vv. 40-43)

1. Reviewed from the past (v. 40)

We know the legs of iron (v. 32) refer to the Roman Empire because it subdued what remained of the Greek Empire and was uniquely strong. It established itself as a world power during the first century B.C. and extended even further than Alexander's conquests. The two legs of the statue indicate the natural division between the eastern and western ends of the empire.

a) Its duration (v. 40*a*)

"The fourth kingdom shall be strong as iron."

In Daniel's day, iron was the strongest metal known. Without question the Roman Empire is the strongest empire the world has ever known. Whereas the Babylonian Empire lasted 70 years and those of Medo-Persia and Greece not much longer than 200 years, the Roman Empire lasted more than 500 years in the West and until A.D. 1453 in the East. No empire has ever come close to its strength and endurance.

b) Its destructiveness (v. 40*b*)

"Forasmuch as iron breaketh into pieces and subdueth all things; and, as iron that breaketh all these, shall it break in pieces and bruise."

All those terms refer to the shattering power of Rome. The Aramaic verb translated "breaketh" means "to crush with a hammer." H. C. Leupold said, "The Roman legions were noted for their ability to crush all resistance with an iron heel. There is apparently little that is constructive in the program of this empire in spite of Roman law and Roman roads and civilization, because the destructive work outweighed all else, for we have the double verb 'crush and demolish' " (*Exposition of Daniel* [Grand Rapids: Baker, 1969], p. 119).

The Romans lasted that long because they ruled with an iron rod. The strong, iron legions of Rome represented the final world power indicated by the image.

2. Revived in the future

There is more to the prophecy: the feet of iron mixed with clay (v. 33). I believe the feet reveal that we will see a return to power of the ancient Roman Empire. Already a timetable has been set for the twelve nations of the European Community, much of whose territory was originally part of the original Roman Empire, to dissolve their economic borders by December 31, 1992 (see the series of articles in the national news magazine *Insight* [20 June 1988]: 8-17).

The *Los Angeles Herald-Examiner* reported back in October 29, 1971, that "the British decision to join the Common Market brought Western Europe to the threshold of its strongest union since the nations involved were tied together as part of the Roman Empire centuries ago" ("Britain's Entry in Market a Step to United Europe," sec. A, p. 4). Commentator Robert Culver wrote, "Two millennia ago, Rome gave the world the ecumenical unity that the League of Nations and the United Nations organizations have sought to revive in our time. . . . [They are] revivals of the ancient Roman ideal that never, since the time of Augustus Caesar, has been wholly lost. It is probable that the *Pax Romana* (Roman peace), the peace of a well-ordered prison with plenty of iron gates, steel doors, trained guards, and high walls, is the best the world will ever achieve till Jesus comes" (*Daniel and the Latter Days* [Chicago: Moody, 1977], p. 125).

Conclusion

The history of the world is reaching its climax. Can America survive? We are succumbing already to the deadly, inevitable deterioration of man. We are a selfish people, and our selfishness will result in self-destruction. Should Jesus tarry, someone else will rise from our ashes and start the cycle all over again.

Focusing on the Facts

1. Why shouldn't the gradual downfall of the United States shock us (see p. 26)?
2. What great period of world history do we see in Daniel 2? What is Israel's basic relationship to that period? Identify the beginning and ending of that period (see pp. 26-27).
3. What enabled Daniel to be elevated to a unique place of authority in Babylon (see p. 27)?
4. What does the phrase "the latter days" refer to (see p. 28)?
5. According to Daniel 2:28-29, what would Nebuchadnezzar learn from his dream (see pp. 28-29)?
6. What about the general appearance of the statue made it a cause for fear (see p. 30)?
7. What do the decreasing densities of the materials in the statue imply about the Gentile world (see p. 30)?
8. What did the image in Nebuchadnezzar's dream represent (see p. 31)?
9. According to verse 37, how did Nebuchadnezzar become "a king of kings" (see p. 32)?
10. Why did God raise up Nebuchadnezzar? What is the significance of the duration of the Babylonian Empire and the captivity of Israel (see p. 32)?
11. What is the significance of Nebuchadnezzar's ruling over "the beasts of the field and the fowls of the heavens" (Dan. 2:38; see pp. 32-33)?
12. How did the gold head relate to Babylon (see p. 33)?
13. Why were no specifics given to Nebuchadnezzar regarding the kingdom that would follow him (see p. 34)?
14. Why was Greece characterized as the empire of bronze (see p. 35)?
15. Under what ruler did Greece "bear rule over all the earth" (Dan. 2:39; see p. 35)?
16. Name a quality of iron that was also characteristic of the Roman Empire (see p. 36).
17. What organization today can be described as a revival of the ancient Roman Empire (see p. 37)?

Pondering the Principles

1. How would you have felt if you had been taken into captivity after the destruction of Jerusalem? What effect would prophecies about a glorious future for Israel have had on you in such a situation? Read the following verses and identify the attribute of God that they display: Exodus 6:4-5; Deuteronomy 7:8-9; Joshua 23:14; Psalm 9:10; 111:5-9; Jeremiah 29:10; 33:14, 20-21. What hope could you share with a Jewish friend to direct his attention to God and to Jesus Christ, the Messiah? Make Psalm 89:1 a reality in your life this week.

2. What part can you play in redirecting the deteriorating course our country is on? Answer these questions: Do you vote? Do you take time to understand the issues and candidates you vote for? Have you ever corresponded with any political representatives? Do you ever pray for them and other influential leaders (1 Tim. 2:1-4)? Do you ever interact with unbelievers and share Scripture with them? Should you be involved on a community team or committee that might benefit from your biblical perspectives? Make the commitment not to be one of the many who say, "Someone else will do it. I'm too busy."

3

The Rise and Fall of the World—Part 2

Outline

Introduction
A. An Analysis of Several World Problems
1. The nuclear arms race
2. The strain in the Western alliance
3. The perpetual retreat of the United States
4. The stress on money and machines
5. The secularism of Western universities
6. The retreat of Christianity
B. An Attempt to Secure World Peace

Review
I. The Dream Received (vv. 1-30)
II. The Dream Recalled (vv. 31-35)
III. The Dream Revealed (vv. 36-45)
A. Babylon (vv. 37-38)
B. Medo-Persia (v. 39a)
C. Greece (v. 39b)
D. Rome (vv. 40-43)
1. Reviewed from the past (v. 40)

Lesson
2. Revived in the future (vv. 41-43)
a) Its deficiency
b) Its division
c) Its duration
d) Its dictator

Conclusion

Introduction

The late Dr. Charles Malik was a native of Lebanon, raised in the Eastern Orthodox church in the midst of an Islamic world. He was one of the founders of the United Nations' Universal Declaration on Human Rights in 1948 and was at one time his country's ambassador to the United States and to the United Nations. In the United Nations Dr. Malik served as President of the General Assembly and President of the Security Council. A graduate of Harvard University, where he earned an M.A. and a Ph.D., he was a visiting professor there as well as a resident professor at the American University in Beirut.

In late 1979 Dr. Malik gave an address titled "The State of the World" at a pastors' advisory committee I attended in Arrowhead Springs. Malik believed that unless something dramatic happened, the world was on the brink of disaster. He gave a lengthy list of the crucial issues facing America and the Western world as we enter the most chaotic period of our history.

A. An Analysis of Several World Problems

1. The nuclear arms race

   Dr. Malik called the nuclear arms race "the balance of terror" because it has the potential to end the world if the wrong man pushes the right button.

2. The strain in the Western alliance

   Dr. Malik also said that America has not done well in maintaining its European ties. He saw the Soviet Union as gradually wooing the American allies in Europe so that they would be more prone to listen to it than to the United States. There is a low level of commitment between us and our allies compared to what we once had, and he believed that that is bringing Soviet power closer to engulfing the world.

3. The perpetual retreat of the United States

   Dr. Malik said that America has continuously retreated from equality with its sworn enemies, and at that time he observed it was standing in a position of weakness in the world.

4. The stress on money and machines

Dr. Malik also said that the West worships the great "gods" of mechanization, progress, technology, and modernization—idols made by our own hands. He pointed out that in recent years we have tried to buy friendship and affinity around the world with money and machines apart from a loving concern for people. He said the only time he could find America sharing community of spirit with a foreign nation was through the efforts of obscure missionaries.

5. The secularism of Western universities

From Dr. Malik's perspective, the main problem facing the world today is the Western university system, in which all the world's policy makers have been educated. He criticized it as being humanistic, Freudian, naturalistic, secularistic, atheistic, and cynical—one that knows nothing about God, absolute standards, or commitment to truth. He said that when a man like the Ayatollah Khomeini rises to power, no one in the West understands his motivation because no one knows what it means to be committed to absolutes.

6. The retreat of Christianity

Dr. Malik then pointed to three major revivals that have occurred in the world recently. One is the revival of atheism, which is sweeping through the East, through Europe, and through other parts of the world. There is also a revival of Judaism in the Zionist movement. And the third is the revival of Islam, which will sweep across the world if it continues at its present rate. Dr. Malik concluded that Christian truth no longer makes a significant impact on the world. He saw it as playing no part in the politics of the Western world. Biblical Christianity in Europe is almost nonexistent, whereas Christianity in America is fading into liberalism as well as secularism.

B. An Attempt to Secure World Peace

After his analysis of the decay of western civilization, Dr. Malik said something that shocked me, especially since he professed to be a Christian. He said that the only hope for the Western world lies in an alliance between the Roman Catholic Church (one of the greatest unifying factors in Europe) and the Eastern Orthodox church (which controls the western front of the Middle East). He believed that if those two powers don't solidify their control politically, Islam will march across Europe. Therefore he called for all Protestant Christians around the globe to join hands with the Pope so that the Christian world will be unified.

It is clear that Malik saw the globe in an imbalance: Islam and the East on the rise while the West wanes because a loss of absolutes leads to dissolution. He saw the Roman Catholic church as a common factor in Europe and North and South America and suggested it could provide the necessary unification to strengthen the Western world. Dr. Malik was particularly concerned that the West declare the eastern Mediterranean (Greece, Turkey, Cyprus, Syria, Lebanon, Israel, Jordan, and Egypt) as part of its domain.

That part of the world once belonged to Rome. And the prophet Daniel said that someday the Roman Empire would be revived (Dan. 2:41-43; 7:19-26). The things Dr. Malik said illustrate how fast we are moving toward the fulfillment of Daniel 2.

Daniel lived six hundred years before Christ, yet he outlined the course of history, even up to our own lifetime. We shouldn't be shocked at that. The Old Testament prophesied the destruction of Babylon (Isa. 13:19-22), Egypt (Ezek. 30:13-16), Tyre (Ezek. 26:1–28:19), and Sidon (Ezek. 28:21-23); and they were destroyed exactly as foretold. It also prophesied that a man named Cyrus would release Israel from captivity (Isa. 45:1, 13), and about two hundred years later he did (Ezra 1:1-4). One of the greatest proofs of the Bible's divine inspiration is fulfilled prophecy, because the prophecies are externally verified in human history.

44

Review

I. THE DREAM RECEIVED (vv. 1-30; see pp. 28-29)

Every power and nation assumes it will exist forever—or at least hopes it will. One such nation was Babylon, technically known as the Neo-Babylonian Empire. Its first great king was Nebuchadnezzar, who received an important dream from God about the future kingdoms of the world.

II. THE DREAM RECALLED (vv. 31-35; see pp. 29-31)

III. THE DREAM REVEALED (vv. 36-45)

Daniel explained the meaning of the dream. He told Nebuchadnezzar that he had seen a large statue representing four great world kingdoms, the first of which he himself ruled.

A. Babylon (vv. 37-38; see pp. 32-33)

This empire lasted about seventy years and came to an end when the Medo-Persians invaded one night and devastated the Babylonians.

B. Medo-Persia (v. 39a; see pp. 33-34)

Because of the two-fold division of the Medes and the Persians, this empire is represented by the statue's chest and arms (v. 32).

C. Greece (v. 39b; see pp. 34-35)

Nebuchadnezzar's dream predicted that Greece would "bear rule over all the earth." And Alexander the Great extended his empire from western Europe to India—an incredible feat for a man who lived only thirty-three years. After Alexander died, his empire was divided among his four generals.

D. Rome (vv. 40-43)

1. Reviewed from the past (v. 40; see pp. 36-37)

The fourth empire revealed in the dream had the strength of iron: "As iron breaketh in pieces and subdueth all things . . . shall it break in pieces and bruise." The legions of the Roman Empire extended everywhere, trampling the known world into submission.

Lesson

2. Revived in the future (vv. 41-43; see p. 37)

"Whereas thou sawest the feet and toes, part of potters' clay and part of iron, the kingdom shall be divided; but there shall be in it of the strength of the iron, forasmuch as thou sawest the iron mixed with miry clay. And as the toes of the feet were part of iron and part of clay, so the kingdom shall be partly strong and partly broken [brittle]. And whereas thou sawest iron mixed with miry clay, they shall mingle themselves with the seed of men, but they shall not adhere one to another, even as iron is not mixed with clay."

a) Its deficiency

The feet of iron and clay imply that the revived Roman Empire will be weak and vulnerable. That's because it will be composed both of what is firm and what is brittle. The original Roman Empire was strong in that its government was solidly organized, its armies well-disciplined, and its policies well-defined, as evidenced by the *Pax Romana*—the Roman peace. But weakness will characterize the future Roman Empire. That's because the weakness is not located in the legs (like ancient Rome), but in the feet.

Verse 43 identifies the weakness as the mingling that will take place with "the seed of men." Scholars have attempted various suggestions, but I believe it simply refers to human beings. The problem in the final

46

form of the Roman Empire is that there will be too many rulers; solidarity will be missing. At the top of the image is the gold head—the only part of the image identified as a ruler and not as an empire. The Babylonian Empire possessed a unique solidarity because one man had complete control. The increasingly diverse authority of the other empires represented by the statue implies that the more decentralized government becomes, the more susceptible it is to internal problems. As soon as government becomes diverse enough to give people the power to vote themselves inordinate amounts of money from the public treasury, the people, through their selfishness, can destroy democracy.

The diversity of the revived Roman Empire will be its destruction. It won't have the solidarity that the Roman Empire once had. Rather, it will be a confederacy, and its power will be distributed among too many people.

b) Its division

The final form of the Roman Empire will have a tenfold division, represented by the ten toes of the image (Dan. 2:41). The ten toes of the image and the ten kings (Dan. 7:24) indicate that the final form of the Roman Empire will be a ten-nation confederacy. God doesn't arbitrarily invent meaningless numbers. The same number is used the same way in Revelation 17:12.

c) Its duration

In the years since the Roman Empire there has never been another world empire. Napoleon tried it, Hitler tried it; and neither of them could do it. Now the Soviet Union has tried it and fortunately has been unsuccessful. Revelation 13:12 tells us of a beast that is mortally wounded but rises again. I believe that's a picture of Rome's death and subsequent revival. In its final form the Roman Empire will consist of ten nations, perhaps represented by the European Community or something like it.

47

d) Its dictator

The Bible tells us that out of the ten-nation confederacy there will arise one ruler, called the "little horn" in Daniel 7:8. He is also called "that man of sin . . . the son of perdition" (2 Thess. 2:3) and the "antichrist" (1 John 2:18). He will be a great world ruler who will pull together the ten-nation coalition. That eventually will provoke the great battle of Armageddon. Watch Europe—it will rise again. Once the ten-nation confederacy takes its form and the Antichrist establishes his rule, it won't be long until the prophetic stone smashes all opposition and fills the whole earth (Dan. 2:35). That stone is none other than Jesus Christ.

Conclusion

We've learned that there will be a succession of world dominions from Nebuchadnezzar to the return of Christ. The Old Testament never described any world powers during the time between the two Roman empires. However, Daniel did differentiate between the legs of iron and the feet made of iron and clay to indicate the weakness of the empire's final form. The ten-nation confederacy, under the rule of the Antichrist, will fight against Christ and attempt to prevent Him from establishing His kingdom. But the battle won't last very long because Christ will crush the dominions of Satan and the world. Christ's kingdom *is* coming. How exciting it is to be alive in a day when we can see those things on the horizon!

I am reminded of the hymn "Lo! He Comes" by Charles Wesley:

> Lo! He comes, with clouds descending,
> Once for our salvation slain;
> Thousand thousand saints attending,
> Swell the triumph of His train:
> Alleluia, alleluia!
> God appears on earth to reign.

Ev'ry eye shall now behold Him,
Robed in dreadful majesty;
Those who set at naught and sold Him,
Pierced and nailed Him to the tree,
Deeply wailing, deeply wailing,
Shall the true Messiah see.

Now the Savior, long expected,
See, in solemn pomp appear;
All His saints, by man rejected,
Now shall meet Him in the air:
Alleluia, alleluia!
See the day of God appear.

Yea, amen! let all adore Thee,
High on Thine eternal throne;
Savior, take the pow'r and glory,
Claim the kingdom for Thine own:
O come quickly, O come quickly,
Alleluia! come, Lord, come!

Focusing on the Facts

1. Why did Dr. Malik conclude that the Western university system is one of the most serious problems facing the world (see p. 43)?
2. What is the condition of Christianity in Europe, and in what direction is it heading in America (see p. 43)?
3. What is one of the Bible's greatest proofs of divine inspiration? Why (see p. 44)?
4. What do the feet of iron and clay seem to indicate about the revived Roman Empire (see p. 46)?
5. Describe the weakness of the final form of the Roman Empire (see pp. 46-47).
6. What do the ten toes of the statue represent when compared with Daniel 7:24 and Revelation 17:12 (see p. 47)?
7. Who will be the dictator of the ten-nation confederacy (see p. 48)?
8. Did the Old Testament reveal the time gap between the two empires of Rome? How did it hint that there would be two different empires (see p. 48)?

Pondering the Principles

1. Do you agree or disagree with Dr. Malik's analysis of the crucial issues facing America and the West? Why or why not? Do you agree with his proposed solution for unification? Why or why not? Of the six areas Dr. Malik mentioned, determine the ones that affect you either directly or indirectly and determine to uphold biblical truth whenever given the opportunity.

2. Meditate on Psalm 2. Praise God that His Messiah shall be victorious over all opposition. Thank Him for the joy that comes from putting your trust in His Son.

4

The Rise and Fall of the World—Part 3

Outline

Introduction
A. The Historical Past of Jerusalem
  1. Its duration through the years
    a) In the days of Abraham
    b) In the days of Joshua
    c) In the days of David
    d) In the days of Jesus
  2. Its destruction by the Babylonians
    a) The cause
    b) The consequence
  3. Its domination by the Gentiles
    a) Jesus' prophecy
      (1) Luke 21:24
      (2) Matthew 23:37-39
    b) The Jewish presence
      (1) After the Babylonian Captivity
      (2) After the Roman destruction
      (3) After the Six-Day War
B. The Prophetical Future of Jerusalem
  1. Zechariah 12:2
  2. Zechariah 14:1-4

Review
 I. The Dream Received (vv. 1-30)
 II. The Dream Recalled (vv. 31-35)
III. The Dream Revealed (vv. 36-45)
  A. Babylon (vv. 37-38)
  B. Medo-Persia (v. 39a)
  C. Greece (v. 39b)
  D. Rome (vv. 40-43)

Lesson

E. The Kingdom of God (vv. 44-45)
  1. Its establishment (v. 44*a*)
    a) Amillennialism
    b) Premillennialism
      (1) Revelation 17:12
      (2) Daniel 7
  2. Its character (v. 44*b*)
  3. Its founder (v. 45)
    a) His identity
      (1) Isaiah 9:6
      (2) Revelation 5:1-10
      (3) Genesis 49:24
      (4) Psalm 118:22
      (5) Isaiah 28:16
      (6) 1 Corinthians 10:4
      (7) Zechariah 14:4
    b) His divinity
    c) His superiority
      (1) The great mountain
      (2) A supernatural stone
      (3) A mighty wind
IV. Daniel Rewarded (vv. 46-49)
  A. The Praise (vv. 46-47)
  B. The Promotion (vv. 48-49)

Conclusion

Introduction

The city of Jerusalem has been a focal point of the world for many years. Even those who don't understand its significance can't help but be amazed by that. The Bible says that Jerusalem is a special place—there's no city like it in the world. Throughout history it has been at center stage in the drama of redemption.

The context of the book of Daniel is the Babylonian Captivity, when the Jewish people were captives in the land of Babylon. Psalm 137:5-6 shows their devotion to Jerusalem: "If I forget thee, O Jerusalem, let my right hand forget her cunning. If I do not remember thee, let my tongue cleave to the roof of my mouth, if I prefer not Jerusalem above my chief joy." The people would sacrifice anything before losing their love for Jerusalem.

What accounts for such commitment to a city? What motivated Nehemiah to return after seventy years and rebuild the walls of Jerusalem (Neh. 1-6)? Why have so many Jewish people emigrated to the land in recent years?

A. The Historical Past of Jerusalem

   1. Its duration through the years

      a) In the days of Abraham

         The first time Jerusalem is mentioned in the Bible is back in Genesis 14:18. At that time the city wasn't called Jerusalem, but Salem. Salem, which means "peace," was most likely an ancient name for the city. Later it became known as Jeru*salem*.

         Mount Moriah, a famous mountain in the middle of the city, was where Abraham prepared to sacrifice his son Isaac before God intervened and provided a ram. How fitting it is that before the city became the center of redemption, God established it as a place where He had provided a sacrifice.

      b) In the days of Joshua

         The first specific reference to Jerusalem is in Joshua 10. Joshua had led the children of Israel into the Promised Land. To them Jerusalem was just one more city to conquer, like Ai and Jericho. But God had set His affection on that city and had great plans for its future.

         Jerusalem is situated on a plateau, surrounded on three sides by valleys three to four hundred feet deep. As such Jerusalem had its own natural defenses. With only its north side on the same level as the surrounding topography, it was a relatively easy city to defend since there was only one way an enemy could attack it. It eventually became the possession of the Israelites.

c) In the days of David

Not much is said about Jerusalem until David became king. Having reigned seven years in Hebron, about twenty miles south of Jerusalem in a valley that was difficult to defend, David decided to move the capital to Jerusalem (2 Sam. 5:7). Jerusalem became the royal capital where David reigned for another thirty-three years. Also known as Mount Zion because of the hill on which the city of David stood, Jerusalem became the political, economic, religious, and social center of Jewish life.

d) In the days of Jesus

Jerusalem became the center of God's redemptive plan at the birth of Jesus. Just down the road from Jerusalem is Bethlehem, the place of the Messiah's birth. And just outside the city walls He died and rose again. At His return He will descend from heaven next to Jerusalem on the Mount of Olives. Then He will enter the city and establish His throne.

2. Its destruction by the Babylonians

a) The cause

Unfortunately, the city God chose as the center for redemptive history became the object of misdirected zeal. When Israel departed from faith in God and was taken into captivity, it became obvious that the people had done well in remembering Jerusalem but had done poorly in remembering what made Jerusalem great. They recalled their love for the city but had forgotten the place of God in their lives. That's why God allowed the city to be destroyed and its people to be taken into captivity.

b) The consequence

Nebuchadnezzar, the powerful monarch of the Babylonian Empire, completely destroyed Jerusalem, making captives of its citizens as well as people in Judah. Jeremiah 52:12-15 records the overthrow of Jerusalem: "In the fifth month, in the tenth day of the month, which was the nineteenth year of Nebuchadnezzar, king of Babylon, came Nebuzaradan, captain of the guard, who served the king of Babylon, into Jerusalem, and burned the house of the Lord, and the king's house; and all the houses of Jerusalem, and all the houses of the great men, burned he with fire. And all the army of the Chaldeans, that were with the captain of the guard, broke down all the walls of Jerusalem round about. Then Nebuzaradan, the captain of the guard, carried away captive certain of the poor of the people, and the residue of the people who remained in the city, and those who fell away, who fell to the king of Babylon, and the rest of the multitude." However the captain left a few vine-dressers and farmers to make sure the king received some product from land (v. 16).

Nebuchadnezzar obviously had two objectives in mind: By destroying the Temple, he assumed he could break the back of the Jewish religion. And by destroying the palace he nullified Judah's political order. In 586 B.C. he succeeded, and so ended a great era.

3. Its domination by the Gentiles

    a) Jesus' prophecy

        (1) Luke 21:24—The Babylonian Captivity was the beginning of what our Lord called "the times of the Gentiles." Specifically He said, "Jerusalem shall be trodden down by the Gentiles, until the times of the Gentiles be fulfilled." Jerusalem was initially trodden down by Nebuchadnezzar. Jesus said it will remain downtrodden until the times of the Gentiles come to an end.

        (2) Matthew 23:37-39—Jesus here reiterated the same prophecy: "O Jerusalem, Jerusalem, thou that killest the prophets, and stonest them who are sent unto thee, how often would I have gathered thy children together, even as a hen gathereth her chickens under her wings, and ye would

not! Behold, your house is left unto you desolate. For I say unto you, Ye shall not see me henceforth, till ye shall say, Blessed is he that cometh in the name of the Lord."

The Lord was saying that Jerusalem would remain desolate until the Jewish people recognized Him as their Messiah when He returned to set up His kingdom. The "times of the Gentiles" will end with the return of Christ. The people will look upon Him whom they have pierced, and "mourn for him, as one mourneth for his only son" (Zech. 12:10) and say, "Blessed is He that cometh in the name of the Lord" (Matt. 23:39). That is why I believe there will be a tremendous revival among the Jewish people during the Great Tribulation prior to Christ's second coming (Rev. 7:4-8; 14:1-3).

b) The Jewish presence

(1) After the Babylonian Captivity

Some of the people returned to Jerusalem after the Babylonian Captivity during the reign of the Medo-Persians and tried to rebuild the city. But they never had the freedom and autonomy they had had previously. After the Medo-Persians, Israel fell under the control of the Greeks, represented by the Seleucids and Maccabeans, under whom they experienced a small degree of liberty. But they lost that liberty when the Romans took charge and made them a vassal state. Even their Idumean kings, the Herods, were nothing but servants of Rome.

(2) After the Roman destruction

In A.D. 70 Titus, son of Emperor Vespasian, brought his Roman legions into Jerusalem and destroyed it again. The first-century Jewish historian Josephus said that the Romans killed 1.1 million Jews in that massacre (*Wars* 6.9.3). Yet after that devastation the surviving Jews continued to pray for the restoration of their city. They congregated at the ruins of the Temple, meeting in the morning, afternoon, and evening. It became such a familiar place of prayer that it was named "The Wailing Wall." Since then the city has been controlled by different Gentile peoples: Romans, Arabs, Turks, and British.

(3) After the Six-Day War

Although Israel became a nation in 1948, they never recovered full access to Jerusalem until they broke through Jordanian resistance on Wednesday, June 7, 1967, during the Six-Day War. It could be said that the Jewish people had prayed for 2,000 years for the moment they arrived at the Wailing Wall and began to shout and pray.

Have the Times of the Gentiles Come to an End?

Some people believe Gentile dominion over the Jewish nation has ended because Israelites head their government. However the Jewish people do not believe they have absolute autonomy in their land; they feel the burden of Gentile oppression, symbolized by restraints imposed by the United Nations. One of the symbols of continuing Gentile dominion is the Dome of the Rock mosque that sits where the Temple once stood. But the Jewish people can't do a thing about replacing it without escalating war in the Middle East.

B. The Prophetical Future of Jerusalem

Clearly Israel is not free from Gentile dominion. And in the future there will be a Gentile invasion of Israel.

1. Zechariah 12:2—The Lord said, "Behold, I will make Jerusalem a cup of trembling unto all the peoples round about, when they shall be in the siege both against Judah and against Jerusalem."

2. Zechariah 14:1-4—"Behold, the day of the Lord cometh, and . . . I will gather all nations against Jerusalem to

battle; and the city shall be taken, and the houses rifled, and the women ravished; and half of the city shall go forth into captivity, and the residue of the people shall not be cut off from the city. Then shall the Lord go forth, and fight against those nations, as when he fought in the day of battle. And his feet shall stand in that day upon the Mount of Olives, which is before Jerusalem on the east, and the Mount of Olives shall cleave in its midst toward the east and toward the west." That is a description of the second coming of Christ. But prior to that the nations will gather against Jerusalem. As a result of the ensuing battle, blood will be as deep as horses' bridles for 200 miles (Rev. 14:20).

The peace of Jerusalem has not yet come. And the peace of Israel awaits the peace of Jerusalem.

Review

I. THE DREAM RECEIVED (vv. 1-30; see pp. 28-29)

II. THE DREAM RECALLED (vv. 31-35; see pp. 29-31)

III. THE DREAM REVEALED (vv. 36-45)

    A. Babylon (vv. 37-38; see pp. 32-33)

    B. Medo-Persia (v. 39*a*; see pp. 33-34)

    C. Greece (v. 39*b*; see pp. 34-35)

    D. Rome (vv. 40-43; see pp. 36-37, 46-48)

Lesson

    E. The Kingdom of God (vv. 44-45)

        1. Its establishment (v. 44*a*)

"In the days of these kings shall the God of heaven set up a kingdom."

The commentaries on Daniel that I read agree that this verse describes the founding of the kingdom of God. They express different opinions about how it happens, but it's clear that God is setting up His kingdom. The phrase "in the days of these kings" refers to no specific kings, as the only king mentioned in the context is Nebuchadnezzar (Dan. 2:37). The fact that there doesn't appear to be an obvious antecedent for the kings is handled differently by the two main eschatological perspectives.

a) Amillennialism

Those who do not believe that Jesus Christ will return to earth and reign in a literal thousand-year kingdom are called "amillennialists." They claim that Daniel 2:44 refers to a spiritual kingdom of Christ set up in the hearts of men before the end of the Babylonian, Medo-Persian, Greek, and Roman kingdoms.

Although Christ did come while Rome was still in existence, the amillennial view has an obvious problem: Nebuchadnezzar's dream dealt with kingdoms, but the Aramaic word translated "kings" (*malkayya*) is different from the one translated "kingdoms" (Aram., *malkwata*).

b) Premillennialism

The context reveals that the kings must be the ten toes of the statue's feet (vv. 41-42), which represent ten kings in the final form of the Roman Empire. I believe verse 44 is Daniel's interpretation of the toes in Nebuchadnezzar's dream, a view that is supported elsewhere in Scripture.

(1) Revelation 17:12—"The ten horns . . . are ten kings." The apostle John records similar imagery of ten kings, but they are represented by ten horns.

(2) Daniel 7—Verses 7 and 20 refer to ten horns. Verse 24 interprets them: "The ten horns out of this kingdom are ten kings that shall arise." Daniel saw Gentile world power finalizing itself in a ten-king or nation confederacy. So "in the days of these kings" means that while those ten leaders are in power God will set up His kingdom.

Verse 44 doesn't make sense if it refers to the other four kingdoms. God didn't set up His earthly kingdom during the time of the Babylonian, Medo-Persian, Greek, or Roman kingdoms. God's kingdom has yet to be established on the earth, although in a spiritual sense His kingdom was established during the last of the four empires. However, since the image in Nebuchadnezzar's dream is a political picture of actual earthly kingdoms, I believe the final kingdom must also be political and earthly. It's not likely that a spiritual kingdom would be introduced into a prophecy that deals with actual historical kingdoms.

The economic community of Europe has already been established into a multi-nation confederacy. Given that and the world's indifferent and antagonistic attitude toward God, there's only one thing that must happen before Christ returns: the voice of the archangel with the trump of God (1 Thess. 4:16).

2. Its character (v. 44b)

"A kingdom, which shall never be destroyed; and the kingdom shall not be left to other people, but it shall break in pieces and consume all these kingdoms, and it shall stand forever."

Unlike other kingdoms, the earthly kingdom God establishes will never be destroyed, fade away, or be taken over by another kingdom. On the contrary, it will consume every present kingdom as well as the remnants of past kingdoms.

Some people have taught that this kingdom is the church. But it can't be the church because the Roman Empire continued for centuries after the church began.

Also the church didn't destroy a ten-nation confederacy in Rome. In fact, the Roman Empire lasted longer after Jesus' death than the other empires lasted from the time of Nebuchadnezzar to Jesus. The church didn't bring a dramatic end to anything.

Daniel 2:34-35 tells us that the stone of God's kingdom smashed the image and blew it away like dust. Then the stone filled the whole earth. The church certainly didn't destroy all the nations of the earth. The church didn't put an end to the times of the Gentiles. In spite of the presence of the church, the Roman Empire continued to dominate, especially in A.D. 70 when it destroyed Jerusalem. The kingdom of God as referred to in Daniel 2:44 can't be the church because the church has never overcome Gentile world power. That's why I believe Daniel was referring to the literal, physical, earthly kingdom that God will establish as the times of the Gentiles come to an end (Rev. 20:4-6).

The Old Testament has many references to God's physical, earthly kingdom. It says that Jerusalem will be rebuilt (Zech. 14:9-21), Israel will be restored to the land (Jer. 23:8), and the curse will be lifted (Isa. 11:7-9). There will be an abundance of food (Joel 2:21-27), and there will be health as well as healing (Isa. 29:18). The topography will change, and a new Temple will be built (Ezek. 40-48). Those elements indicate a literal, physical kingdom, although it certainly will have a spiritual reality to it.

3. Its founder (v. 45)

"Forasmuch as thou sawest that the stone was cut out of the mountain without hands, and that it broke in pieces the iron, the bronze, the clay, the silver, and the gold, the great God hath made known to the king what shall come to pass hereafter; and the dream is certain, and the interpretation of it sure."

Verse 45 is Daniel's interpretation of verses 34-35: "Thou sawest until a stone was cut out without hands, which smote the image upon its feet that were of iron and clay, and broke them to pieces. Then were the iron, the clay, the bronze, the silver, and the gold, broken to pieces together, and became like the chaff of the summer threshing floors; and the wind carried them away, that no place was found for them; and the stone that smote the image became a great mountain, and filled the whole earth."

a) His identity

That stone is none other than Jesus Christ—He is the only One who can put an end to the times of the Gentiles and destroy the governments of the world.

   (1) Isaiah 9:6—Isaiah prophesied that "the government shall be upon his shoulder." Christ alone has the right to rule.

   (2) Revelation 5:1-10—Angels searched heaven to find someone worthy to open the scroll of the title deed to the earth. Only Jesus Christ, the Lamb of God, could do it because only He has the right to possess the earth.

   (3) Genesis 49:24—"From thence is the shepherd, the stone of Israel." Here God is referred to as a stone.

   (4) Psalm 118:22—"The stone which the builders refused is become the head of the corner" (cf. 1 Pet. 2:8). Not only did the apostle Peter use this verse in reference to Christ, but also Jesus Himself quoted it (Matt. 21:42).

   (5) Isaiah 28:16—God said, "Behold, I lay in Zion for a foundation a stone, a tested stone, a precious cornerstone, a sure foundation."

   (6) 1 Corinthians 10:4—In speaking of Israel in the wilderness, Paul said, "They drank of that spiritual Rock that followed them, and that Rock was Christ."

   (7) Zechariah 14:4—Christ is the stone that will smash Gentile dominion. At His second coming

His "feet shall stand in that day upon the Mount of Olives [which] shall cleave in its midst toward the east and toward the west, and there shall be a very great valley." Into that valley, called "the valley of decision" (Joel 3:14), will come Gentiles from all over the globe. There they are to be judged by God. After their judgment, God will set up His kingdom in the city of Jerusalem, where Christ will reign for a thousand years before the earth is superseded by the eternal state.

b) His divinity

Daniel 2:45 says this Messianic stone was "cut out of the mountain without hands." That is first of all a reflection of Christ's virgin birth. This stone was not man-made. Second, I believe it is a reflection of Christ's resurrection—no human agency was involved in that. His own power brought Him out of the grave (John 10:18).

c) His superiority

Notice that verse 45 says that the stone smashes the idol's feet—the final empire and the weakest part of the statue. As a result, the entire Gentile reign comes to an end. Although Jesus is a crushing stone (Matt. 21:44), at the same time He is a restoring stone, for no sooner does He smash and crush than He fills the earth (Dan. 2:35).

The cultural background of Nebuchadnezzar's religion highlights the superiority of the stone.

(1) The great mountain

According to archaeologists, Nebuchadnezzar's chief god was called "Bel Marduk," that is, "Marduk *the* god." Sometimes he was associated with a great mountain. The fact that the stone in Nebuchadnezzar's dream became a great mountain (v. 35) led the king to understand that his god would be replaced by the true God.

63

(2) A supernatural stone

> Nebuchadnezzar was one of the great builders in ancient history. (For example, he is credited with the Hanging Gardens of Babylon, one of the seven wonders of the ancient world.) He would have understood the importance of a stone cut out without hands because he was familiar with the incredible effort necessary to cut out stone by hand.

(3) A mighty wind

> Verse 35 says the wind came along after the image had been smashed and blew the pieces away. I believe that also pointed Nebuchadnezzar to the inferiority of his god. In Babylonian theology, Bel Marduk defeated Tiamat, the dragon of chaos, by sending a hurricane into its mouth and blowing it up (Will Durant, *Our Oriental Heritage* [N.Y.: Simon and Schuster, 1954], pp. 236-37).

If anyone were to doubt Daniel's recall of the dream and his interpretation, verse 45 puts those doubts to rest: "The dream is certain, and the interpretation of it sure."

IV. DANIEL REWARDED (vv. 46-49)

A. The Praise (vv. 46-47)

"Then the king, Nebuchadnezzar, fell upon his face, and worshiped Daniel, and commanded that they should offer an oblation and sweet odors unto him. The king answered unto Daniel, and said, Of a truth it is that your God is the God of gods, and the Lord of kings, and a revealer of secrets, seeing thou couldest reveal this secret."

Why would the king worship Daniel? He didn't know Daniel's God, so he figured the only way to get to him was through Daniel. In verse 47 Nebuchadnezzar offered praise to Daniel's God. But his was shallow commitment based on the emotion of the moment, for he abandoned it in the next chapter.

B. The Promotion (vv. 48-49)

> "Then the king made Daniel a great man, and gave him many great gifts, and made him ruler over the whole province of Babylon, and chief of the governors over all the wise men of Babylon. Then Daniel requested of the king, and he set Shadrach, Meshach, and Abed-nego over the affairs of the province of Babylon; but Daniel sat in the gate of the king."

Daniel was promoted to prime minister of the Babylonian Empire. When Daniel received his new position, he had his three friends raised into strategic places to be used by God. Some have denied the authenticity of the book of Daniel on the basis that kings don't bow to their captives. But kings do bow to God. The book of Daniel is the Word of God revealed to Daniel, and Nebuchadnezzar knew it.

Conclusion

The book of Daniel gives us an important principle: you never have to scheme to acquire the position or ministry you desire. Simply obey God. He will open doors and use you in a way far beyond what you ever dreamed (Eph. 3:20-21). Daniel simply obeyed God in every situation He took him through. Daniel became the prime minister of Babylon because God put him there. Since he didn't put himself there, he didn't have to worry about staying there. God would keep Daniel there until he had served His purpose. Don't seek to promote yourself; let God direct your path as you obey His will.

Focusing on the Facts

1. According to Psalm 137, how did the captives of Babylon feel about Jerusalem (see pp. 52-53)?
2. What is the first apparent mention of Jerusalem in the Bible (see p. 53)?
3. What is significant about a particular mountain near the ancient city in the days of Abraham (see p. 53)?

4. What did Jerusalem become under David (see p. 54)?
5. Why did God allow Jerusalem to be destroyed and its people taken into captivity (see p. 54)?
6. What were Nebuchadnezzar's two objectives in destroying Jerusalem (see p. 55)?
7. What period began at the destruction of Jerusalem by Nebuchadnezzar (see p. 55)?
8. According to Jesus, how long will Jerusalem remain desolate (Matt. 23:37-39; see pp. 55-56)?
9. When did the Jewish people finally regain control of Jerusalem (see p. 57)?
10. Why have the times of the Gentiles not yet ended (see p. 57)?
11. What do amillennial scholars believe regarding the kingdom of Christ (see p. 59)?
12. What do the kings of verse 44 seem to refer to (see p. 59)?
13. Why is it logical to assume that the final kingdom must be a political and earthly one (see p. 60)?
14. What will the kingdom God establishes be like? Why can't it be identified with the church (see pp. 60-61)?
15. What identification of Christ in Scripture corresponds with Daniel 2:45 (see pp. 61-62)?
16. What is significant about the great mountain and wind in Nebuchadnezzar's dream (see p. 64)?
17. How was Daniel rewarded for his interpretation (see p. 65)?

Pondering the Principles

1. Many Jewish people made a sad mistake by retaining their love for Jerusalem without continuing to love God. Christians are no different. Revelation 2 records a rebuke of the church at Ephesus, which had left its first love—Jesus Christ (v. 4). Evaluate your own spiritual life. Do you hunger and thirst for righteousness and seek to know Christ intimately? Have you retired from seeking to please God and to be an imitator of Christ? Be refreshed by Paul's zeal to "win Christ" by reading Philippians 3:4-14.

2. It is well known that those who seek success must pay the price. However in the spiritual realm we often fail to implement that same principle, expecting immediate success without sacrifice and struggle. But such success does not exist. Consider Daniel's

promotion granted to him by God. What price did he pay? Consider Jesus in the Garden of Gethsemane as recorded in Luke 22:41-44. What attitude did He manifest in the struggle He had with going to the cross? What happened as a result (v. 43)? The principle of submission before success is a paradox. If you find yourself saying, "Help me through, Lord, and then I'll obey," you have reversed God's order for success. Identify areas in your own life where there is a lack of success or accomplishment. If you find those areas are rooted in a lack of submission to God's revealed will and the subjective leading of His Spirit, commit yourself to obeying God first and trusting Him with the results.

5
How Are the Mighty Fallen!

Outline

Introduction (vv. 1-3)
A. The Condemnation of Pride
    1. Explained
    2. Expressed
        a) Proverbs 21:4
        b) Proverbs 6:17
        c) Proverbs 16:5
        d) Proverbs 8:13
        e) Proverbs 16:18
        f) Proverbs 29:23
        g) Proverbs 11:2
    3. Exemplified
B. The Consequences of Pride
C. The Conversion of Pride
    1. Its process
    2. Its pinnacle

Lesson
I. The Reception of the Dream (vv. 4-8)
    A. Its Impact on Nebuchadnezzar (vv. 4-5)
    B. The Inability of the Wise Men (vv. 6-7)
    C. The Influence of Daniel (v. 8)
        1. God's holiness explained
        2. God's holiness exemplified
II. The Recitation of the Dream (vv. 9-18)
    A. The Ability of Daniel (v. 9)
    B. The Parts of the Dream (vv. 10-17)
        1. The tree (vv. 10-12)
        2. The decree (vv. 13-17)

69

Introduction

A. The Condemnation of Pride

1. Explained

Perhaps the most destructive attitude of all is pride. It has damned not only Satan and his angels, but also men and women throughout history. Pride is worthy of condemnation because it violates the first commandment: to have no other gods before God Himself (Ex. 20:3). God alone is to be worshiped and served because His will is supreme. But pride asserts that man should take supremacy over God. God proclaimed through Isaiah, "My glory I will not give to another" (Isa. 48:11, NASB*). God will not tolerate a usurper who attempts to rise above Him.

* *New American Standard Bible.*

2. Expressed

The book of Proverbs gives us insight into how God feels about pride:

a) Proverbs 21:4—"An high look, and a proud heart . . . are sin."

b) Proverbs 6:17—The Lord hates "a proud look."

c) Proverbs 16:5—"Every one who is proud in heart is an abomination to the Lord."

d) Proverbs 8:13—"The fear of the Lord is to hate evil; pride, and arrogance . . . do I hate."

e) Proverbs 16:18—"Pride goeth before destruction, and an haughty spirit before a fall."

f) Proverbs 29:23—"A man's pride shall bring him low."

g) Proverbs 11:2—"When pride cometh, then cometh shame."

Pride is a serious sin that is condemned repeatedly throughout Scripture. It is an abomination because it desecrates the name of God. And it also brings about destruction because the end of pride is judgment.

3. Exemplified

A specific example of judgment against pride concerns a prophecy about Edom—a territory in the desert southeast of Jerusalem. The city of Petra, Edom's capital, was well fortified. It was nestled between high cliffs, and the only entrance was only wide enough for a single individual to pass through. It could be guarded by just one soldier, making it virtually impenetrable.

Jeremiah 49:16-17 is a prophecy against Edom: "Thy terribleness hath deceived thee, and the pride of thine heart, O thou that dwellest in the clefts of the rock, that holdest the height of the hill; though thou shouldest

71

make thy nest as high as the eagle, I will bring thee down from there, saith the Lord. Also Edom shall be a desolation; every one that goeth by it shall be appalled, and shall hiss at all its plagues." Today Petra is empty. Its destruction came when its water supply, carried by troughs that flowed down the sides of the cliffs, was cut off by its adversaries. Eventually the people had to surrender. God brought that city down from its pride.

B. The Consequences of Pride

James 4:6 summarizes God's response to pride: He "resisteth the proud, but giveth grace unto the humble" (cf. Prov. 3:34). Daniel 4 is a graphic illustration of that truth. It shows the importance of properly recognizing the sovereignty and supremacy of God and the humble state of man. That theme is capsulized in verse 17: "This matter is . . . to the intent that the living may know that the Most High ruleth in the kingdom of men." No man can set himself above God. That same principle is repeated: "The Most High ruleth in the kingdom of men" (v. 25, 32). King Nebuchadnezzar finally got the message: "I blessed the Most High, and I praised and honored him who liveth forever, whose dominion is an everlasting dominion, and his kingdom is from generation to generation"(v. 34).

In Daniel 4 we meet a proud man. Nebuchadnezzar was the monarch of the first of four empires that ruled his part of the world. As king of such a great empire, he became proud and set himself up as God. He had a ninety-foot image of himself built out of gold and forced the people to bow down and worship it (Dan. 3:5). However, when Shadrach, Meshach, and Abednego refused to do so, they were thrown into a fiery furnace (vv. 12, 20). Such was the strength of Nebuchadnezzar's ego. But in Daniel 4 God brings Nebuchadnezzar down and then gives him grace after he humbles himself.

There is more to Daniel 4 than a historical account of Nebuchadnezzar. He stands as a symbol of several things: First, he is a symbol of any leader who exalts himself. He is a warning to all the Shahs, Ayatollahs, Amins, Hitlers, and Mussolinis who pridefully seek to establish their empires in place of God. But he is a warning as well to those of us who desire to rule the little empires we invent within ourselves, in which we crown ourselves king. Nebuchadnezzar also serves as a symbol of how God deals with all the proud empires of the times of the Gentiles. He crushed the Babylonian, Medo-Persian, Greek, and Roman empires and will ultimately destroy the revived Roman Empire before He establishes the kingdom of Christ.

C. The Conversion of Pride

1. Its process

Daniel 4 is the climax of Nebuchadnezzar's spiritual biography. The Lord began His work on him by bringing Daniel and his three friends into his life. When they defied him by not accepting the royal food and drink, he was immediately confronted by their unique integrity, understanding, and wisdom—characteristics superior to those of anyone in his kingdom (Dan. 1). After God established their credibility before the king, He enabled Daniel to solve an incredible dream that no one else in Nebuchadnezzar's kingdom knew about or could interpret (Dan. 2). Struck by Daniel's divinely given capability of knowing and interpreting visions and dreams, Nebuchadnezzar was led to an even deeper understanding of God. When Daniel's three friends refused to obey the decree to worship Nebuchadnezzar's image, they were thrown into a fiery furnace—but were miraculously protected by one "like a son of the gods" (Dan. 3:25). Again Nebuchadnezzar saw God at work.

2. Its pinnacle

In Daniel 4 we see what I believe is Nebuchadnezzar's conversion to faith in the true God. Some commentators have appropriately titled the chapter "The Conversion of Nebuchadnezzar." It relates how God broke his pride by humbling him and then turning his heart toward Him in faith. God did so, in part, through another dream.

Daniel 4:1-3 says, "Nebuchadnezzar, the king, unto all people, nations, and languages that dwell in all the earth: Peace be multiplied unto you. I thought it good to show the signs and wonders that the

High God hath wrought toward me. How great are his signs! And how mighty are his wonders! His kingdom is an everlasting kingdom, and his dominion is from generation to generation." Nebuchadnezzar is the writer of chapter 4. I don't believe he was an inspired author of Scripture, but I do believe God made sure that what Nebuchadnezzar said was accurately recorded by Daniel. The Bible maintains its accuracy by faithfully recording events and conversations. For example, when the devil is quoted in the Bible, he is quoted accurately although what he said may have been false. Therefore, when Nebuchadnezzar gave this testimony, Daniel accurately recorded it under the inspiration of the Holy Spirit.

Nebuchadnezzar recorded his testimony in the first person. As such it is his personal testimony of how he came to believe in God, whom he recognized as being above all the deities of his people.

Lesson

I. THE RECEPTION OF THE DREAM (vv. 4-8)

A. Its Impact on Nebuchadnezzar (vv. 4-5)

"I, Nebuchadnezzar, was at rest in mine house, and flourishing in my palace. I saw a dream which made me afraid, and the thoughts upon my bed and the visions of my head troubled me."

The Aramaic word translated "rest" means that Nebuchadnezzar was free from apprehension and fear. At that time his kingdom had no significant internal problems or serious external opposition. And he was prospering—the Aramaic word translated "flourishing" means that his life was literally "growing green."

Daniel 4 probably took place between the thirtieth and thirty-fifth years of Nebuchadnezzar's reign, approximately twenty-five to thirty years after the incident of the fiery furnace. Daniel was between forty-five and fifty years of age. That was when God gave Nebuchadnezzar a second dream. And the dream panicked him, forcing him out of his peaceful condition. In his fear he summoned help.

B. The Inability of the Wise Men (vv. 6-7)

"Therefore made I a decree to bring in all the wise men of Babylon before me, that they might make known unto me the interpretation of the dream. Then came in the magicians, the astrologers, the Chaldeans, and the soothsayers; and I told the dream to them, but they did not make known unto me its interpretation."

Nebuchadnezzar called upon the court wise men, who were unable to recount and interpret his previous dream (Dan. 2:10-11). Once again they couldn't interpret his dream. Their inability demonstrates the limit and folly of human wisdom to comprehend spiritual truth apart from God. First Corinthians 2:14 says, "The natural man receiveth [understands] not the things of the Spirit of God." Jesus said that God had hidden the truth "from the wise and prudent, and . . . revealed [it] unto babes" (Matt. 11:25). The unbelieving world is "ever learning, and never able to come to the knowledge of the truth" (2 Tim. 3:7).

C. The Influence of Daniel (v. 8)

"But at the last Daniel came in before me, whose name is Belteshazzar, according to the name of my god, and in whom is the spirit of the holy gods [Aram., *elahin*, "gods" or "God"]."

Nebuchadnezzar used Daniel's Babylonian name because his testimony was directed to the Babylonians. Daniel demonstrated a strategic sense of timing when he came to provide the interpretation of the dream after the failure of the wise men.

Throughout the years of his association with Daniel, Nebuchadnezzar came to recognize that the Spirit of God dwelt in him. It was clear that Daniel served a different God than the wise men, because the deities of the Babylonians were not holy. Pagan deities are no better than the men who worship them. But the Holy Spirit indwelt Daniel, and Nebuchadnezzar came to know that was true. By this time Nebuchadnezzar had a fuller understanding of the nature of God than he had ever had before. But how did Nebuchadnezzar know that the God who resided with Daniel was the Holy God?

1. God's holiness explained

Twenty-five or thirty years had passed since Daniel revealed and interpreted the king's first dream. It seems logical to conclude that Daniel, who was the prime minister of Babylon, told Nebuchadnezzar all he could about God in those intervening years. Daniel cared about him.

2. God's holiness exemplified

Nebuchadnezzar also gained an understanding of what God was like by the exemplary life of Daniel. He didn't defile himself with the king's food or wine, nor did he indulge in the immoralities of a pagan society. Daniel lived a pure and a virtuous life. The logical conclusion is that he obeyed a holy and virtuous God, because a man's life reflects the God he worships.

When Henry Stanley found David Livingstone in the heart of Africa, he stayed with him for four months. Apparently Livingstone didn't say much to Stanley about spiritual things—he just continued to be about his business with the Africans. In his exciting account, *How I Found Livingstone*, Stanley wrote, "His religion is not of the theoretical kind, but is a constant, earnest, sincere practice. It is neither demonstrative nor loud, but manifests itself in a quiet practical way. . . . In him religion exhibits its loveliest features; it governs his conduct not only towards his servants but towards the natives . . . and all who come in contact with him" ([N.Y.: C. Scribner, 1913], pp. 428-34). Livingstone was a man of God who permitted the Lord to live through him. Consequently his life was one of victory and blessing. By the sheer influence and impact of his virtue Livingstone directed Stanley to Christ. That is probably what happened between Daniel and Nebuchadnezzar: Daniel not only spoke of the character of God, but manifested it as well.

II. THE RECITATION OF THE DREAM (vv. 9-18)

A. The Ability of Daniel (v. 9)

"O Belteshazzar, master of the magicians, because I know that the spirit of the holy [God] is in thee, and no secret troubleth thee, tell me the visions of my dream that I have seen, and the interpretation of it."

By giving Daniel the highest title he could think of, "master of the magicians," Nebuchadnezzar acknowledged Daniel's superiority to the other wise men. The Aramaic word translated "magicians" is best understood to refer to scholars. Daniel was the chief scholar—the most erudite, knowledgeable, and gifted of the wise men. The name *Daniel* became a byword for knowledge and wisdom. Ezekiel said of the prince of Tyre, "Behold, thou art wiser than Daniel" (Ezek. 28:3). Since Nebuchadnezzar knew that Daniel had incredible knowledge and wisdom and that he possessed the Spirit of God, he knew Daniel could interpret his dream.

B. The Parts of the Dream (vv. 10-17)

1. The tree (vv. 10-12)

"Thus were the visions of mine head in my bed: I saw and, behold, a tree in the midst of the earth, and the height of it was great. The tree grew, and was strong, and its height reached unto heaven, and the sight of it to the end of all the earth. Its leaves were fair, and its fruit much, and in it was food for all; the beasts of the field had shadow under it, and the fowls of the heavens dwelt in its boughs, and all flesh was fed from it."

A huge tree rose out of the earth, providing food and shelter for all.

2. The decree (vv. 13-17)

a) The messenger (v. 13)

"I saw in the visions of my head on my bed, and, behold, a watcher and an holy one came down from heaven."

"A watcher and an holy one" identifies the being as an angel. Those terms emphasize his vigilance and his holiness.

b) The message (vv. 14-16)

"He cried aloud, and said thus: Hew down the tree, and cut off its branches; shake off its leaves, and scatter its fruit; let the beasts get away from under it, and the fowls from its branches. Nevertheless, leave the stump of its roots in the earth, even with a band [fence] of iron and bronze, in the tender grass of the field; and let him be wet with the dew of heaven, and let his portion be with the beasts in the grass of the earth. Let his heart be changed from man's, and let a beast's heart be given unto him; and let seven times pass over him."

The pronouns "him" and "his" indicates that the tree represents a man. The term "heart" refers to the cognitive processes that determine one's actions. The man's mind would become like that of an animal, reminiscent of the unusual psychological delusion known as lycanthropy (Gk., *lukos*, "wolf"; *anthropos*, "man"). The biblical scholar R. K. Harrison recounted this personal experience:

"A great many doctors spend an entire, busy professional career without once encountering an instance of the kind of monomania described in the book of Daniel. The present writer, therefore, considers himself particularly fortunate to have actually observed a clinical case of [lycanthropy] in a British mental institution in 1946. The patient was in his early 20's, who reportedly had been hospitalized for about five years. His symptoms were well developed on admission, and diagnosis was immediate and conclusive.

He was of average height and weight with good physique, and was in excellent bodily health. His mental symptoms included pronounced antisocial tendencies, and because of this he spent the entire day from dawn to dusk outdoors, on the grounds of the institution. . . .

"His daily routine consisted of wandering around the magnificent lawns with which the otherwise dingy hospital situation was graced, and it was his custom to pluck up and eat handfuls of the grass as he went along. On observation he was seen to discriminate carefully between grass and weeds, and on inquiry from the attendant, the writer was told the diet of this patient consisted exclusively of grass from hospital lawns. He never ate institutional food with other inmates, and his only drink was water. . . .

"The writer was able to examine him cursorily, and the only physical abnormality noted consisted of a lengthening of the hair and a coarse, thickened condition of the finger-nails. Without institutional care, the patient would have manifested precisely the same physical conditions as those mentioned in Daniel 4:33" (*Introduction to the Old Testament* [Grand Rapids: Eerdmans, 1969], pp. 1116-17).

The actions of the man reported in Nebuchadnezzar's dream are not an unknown psychological phenomenon. However, in this case it was induced by God.

c) The meaning (v. 17)

"This matter is by the decree of the watchers, and the demand by the word of the holy ones, to the intent that the living may know that the Most High ruleth in the kingdom of men, and giveth it to whomsoever he will, and setteth up over it the basest of men."

Evidently there was more than one angel. Their message was that God sovereignly rules over men and superintends their earthly reigns.

C. The Request of Nebuchadnezzar (v. 18)

"This dream I, King Nebuchadnezzar, have seen. Now thou, O Belteshazzar, declare the interpretation of it, forasmuch as all the wise men of my kingdom are not able to make known unto me the interpretation; but thou art able; for the spirit of the holy [God] is in thee."

Daniel stood out in his society because he had a Spirit-controlled life.

III. THE REVELATION OF THE DREAM (vv. 19-27)

A. The Compassion of Daniel (v. 19)

1. His attitude (v. 19a)

"Then Daniel, whose name was Belteshazzar, was perplexed for one hour, and his thoughts troubled him."

The "one hour" was probably not a literal hour. The Aramaic phrase means "for a little while." Daniel's thoughts troubled him, not because he didn't know how to interpret the dream, but because of its grave implications toward Nebuchadnezzar.

2. His answer (v. 19b)

"The king spoke, and said, Belteshazzar, let not the dream, or its interpretation, trouble thee. Belteshazzar answered and said, My lord, the dream be to them that hate thee, and the interpretation of it to thine enemies."

Daniel wished that what he had to say was true of Nebuchadnezzar's enemies and not of him. His restraint probably proved to Nebuchadnezzar that he loved him. If he had blurted out the condemnation, Nebuchadnezzar might have questioned Daniel's compassion. But his restraint proved how deeply he cared. And that is a great lesson. We know the message of salvation is also a message of judgment, but we should never preach it with a vindictive heart. We should never talk to people about the loss of their eternal souls without a sense of sadness and compassion. Daniel hurt inside because he had to tell the king something he didn't want to tell him.

B. The Confrontation by Daniel (vv. 20-26)

1. A parallel in history (vv. 20-22)

"The tree that thou sawest, which grew, and was strong, whose height reached unto the heaven, and the sight of it to all the earth, whose leaves were fair, and its fruit much, and in it was food for all; under which the beasts of the field dwelt, and upon whose branches the fowls of the heaven had their habitation: It is thou, O king."

When Nathan confronted David's sin he said, "Thou art the man" (2 Sam. 12:7). Daniel confronted Nebuchadnezzar in much the same way. Most preachers would back down in a crisis like this one, but Daniel didn't.

2. A lesson in humility (vv. 23-25)

"Whereas the king saw a watcher and an holy one coming down from heaven, and saying, Hew the tree down, and destroy it; yet leave the stump of its roots in the earth, even with a band [fence] of iron and bronze, in the tender grass of the field; and let him be wet with the dew of heaven, and let his portion be with the beasts of the field, till seven times pass over him; this is the interpretation, O king, and this is the decree of the Most High, which is come upon my lord, the king: That they shall drive thee from men, and thy dwelling shall be with the beasts of the field, and they shall make thee to eat grass [lit. "herbage"] like oxen, and they shall wet thee with the dew of heaven, and seven times [years] shall pass over thee, till thou know that the Most High ruleth in the kingdom of men, and giveth it to whomsoever he will."

Nebuchadnezzar would be humiliated for seven years. He would become insane and act like an animal.

3. A ray of hope (v. 26)

"Whereas they commanded to leave the stump of the tree roots, thy kingdom shall be sure unto thee, after thou shalt have known that the heavens do rule."

That the tree stump remained indicated Nebuchadnezzar wouldn't die. After seven years he would reclaim his throne once again, but only after learning that every kingdom belongs to God, the ruler of everything. Any man who rules a kingdom does so only because God has allowed him to.

C. The Counsel of Daniel (v. 27)

"Wherefore, O king, let my counsel be acceptable unto thee, and break off thy sins by righteousness, and thine iniquities by showing mercy to the poor, if there may be a lengthening of thy tranquillity."

The proof of the king's righteousness would be good deeds to those in need. Daniel was calling for Nebuchadnezzar to repent of his sin, enter into a righteous relationship with God, and begin to live a merciful life. Such a confrontation was particularly appropriate for Nebuchadnezzar, for he had been a merciless, murderous king.

Yet in spite of the dream and its interpretation, Nebuchadnezzar refused to repent. He responded to Daniel's admonition like Felix, the Roman procurator of Judea, responded to the apostle Paul's: "When I have a convenient season, I will call for thee" (Acts 24:25). Nebuchadnezzar postponed dealing with the issue. Yet if he had repented, God wouldn't have judged him. God said He would destroy Nineveh, but Nineveh repented and He didn't. God may warn of coming judgment, but when one repents, He turns from His judgment.

IV. THE REALIZATION OF THE DREAM (vv. 28-33)

A. The Patience of God (vv. 28-29a)

"All this came upon the king, Nebuchadnezzar. At the end of twelve months . . ."

God is a patient, gracious God. He gave Nebuchadnezzar a year to respond to Daniel's appeal and straighten out his life.

B. The Pride of Nebuchadnezzar (vv. 29b-30)

"He walked in the palace of the kingdom of Babylon. The king spoke, and said, Is not this great Babylon, that I have built for the house of the kingdom by the might of my power, and for the honor of my majesty?"

His extreme pride manifested itself as he boasted about *his* Babylon, the largest and most powerful city of antiquity.

C. The Punishment by God (vv. 31-33)

"While the word was in the king's mouth, there fell a voice from heaven, saying, O King Nebuchadnezzar, to thee it is spoken. The kingdom is departed from thee. And they shall drive thee from men, and thy dwelling shall be with the beasts of the field; they shall make thee to eat grass like oxen, and seven times shall pass over thee, until thou know that the Most High ruleth in the kingdom of men, and giveth it to whomsoever he will. The same hour was the thing fulfilled upon Nebuchadnezzar, and he was driven from men, and did eat grass like oxen, and his body was wet with the dew of heaven, till his hairs were grown like eagles' feathers, and his nails like birds' claws."

What an incredible picture! The great king was outside where everyone could see him. He crawled about like an animal, eating grass. He became a raving maniac for seven years. His unkempt hair resembled the feathers of an eagle and his nails the talons of a bird.

Under such conditions, there were probably many underlings who wanted to take over Nebuchadnezzar's rule. But God never let one ambitious noble lay a hand on his throne because He had promised Nebuchadnezzar that he would return to it. After Nebuchadnezzar's death there was much political intrigue surrounding the throne. But for seven years while he was a raving maniac, no one took over Nebuchadnezzar's throne. I believe God used Daniel to secure and control it until it could be given back to the king.

V. THE RESTORATION OF NEBUCHADNEZZAR (vv. 34-37)

A. An Expression of Repentance (vv. 34-35)

"At the end of the days I, Nebuchadnezzar, lifted up mine eyes unto heaven, and mine understanding returned unto me, and I blessed the Most High, and I praised and honored him who liveth forever, whose dominion is an everlasting dominion, and his kingdom is from generation to generation. And all the inhabitants of the earth are reputed as nothing; and he doeth according to his will in the army of heaven, and among the inhabitants of the earth, and none can stay his hand, or say unto him, What doest thou?"

Nebuchadnezzar finally understood God's message. What a transformation! God can save the high and the mighty if they humble themselves. God will humble everyone someday, so it is advisable to be humbled while having the opportunity to accept His grace.

B. An Explanation of Restoration (vv. 36-37)

1. His returned reason (v. 36)

"At the same time my reason returned unto me; and for the glory of my kingdom, mine honor and brightness returned unto me; and my counselors and my lords sought unto me; and I was established in my kingdom, and excellent majesty was added unto me."

After his reason had returned, he not only regained his former glory, but surpassed it as well. Even his counselors and lords sought him out and accepted him.

2. His right reaction (v. 37)

"Now I, Nebuchadnezzar, praise and extol and honor the King of heaven, all whose works are truth, and his ways justice; and those that walk in pride he is able to abase [humble]."

I believe you'll find Nebuchadnezzar in heaven. Clearly he learned that God resists the proud and gives grace to the humble.

Focusing on the Facts

1. Why is God alone to be worshiped and served? In spite of that, what does pride assert (see p. 70)?
2. What does Proverbs teach about pride (see p. 71)?
3. Explain how God responds to the proud and the humble (James 4:6; see p. 72).
4. Daniel 4 is a warning against pride. To whom is it explicitly and implicitly directed (see p. 72)?
5. How had God been progressively working in Nebuchadnezzar's life in the first three chapters of Daniel (see p. 73)?
6. Since Nebuchadnezzar essentially wrote Daniel 4, yet wasn't divinely inspired, how could it be an accurate, trustworthy account (see p. 74)?
7. What was the condition of Nebuchadnezzar's kingdom at the outset of his testimony (Dan. 4:4; see p. 74)?
8. Why did Nebuchadnezzar summon his wise men (see p. 75)?
9. What did Daniel possess that the other wise men didn't (see p. 75)?
10. How did Nebuchadnezzar know that the holy God resided with Daniel (see p. 76)?
11. According to Daniel 4:9, what was Nebuchadnezzar clearly convinced of? (see p. 77)?
12. What is a legitimate clinical explanation for the divinely effected transformation that Nebuchadnezzar experienced (see p. 78)?
13. According to Daniel 4:17, why did Nebuchadnezzar become insane (see p. 79)?
14. Why was Daniel "perplexed" about the interpretation of the dream (Dan. 4:19; see p. 80)?
15. What was symbolic about the stump left in the ground (see p. 82)?
16. What was Daniel's counsel to the king (Dan. 4:27; see p. 82)?
17. How did God demonstrate His patience with Nebuchadnezzar (Dan. 4:29; see pp. 82-83)?
18. What was restored to Nebuchadnezzar after seven years (see p. 84)?

Pondering the Principles

1. We have seen that God used Daniel over a period of forty years to lead Nebuchadnezzar to faith in Him. Often by the time someone finally comes to Christ, many people will have influenced that person with spiritual truth. What people played a part in your progress toward salvation? Consider calling or writing them to express your appreciation for their concern. Are you currently seeking to influence others for Christ? If not, choose someone in your sphere of influence who needs to be introduced to the Most High God.

2. By the sheer influence and impact of his virtuous life, David Livingstone pointed Stanley to Christ. Since actions speak louder than words, take some time to evaluate your actions. Do they reflect the righteousness of Christ? Are they easily understood as coming from pure motives? Do they express your faith in a risen Lord as well as your hope in a returning Lord? If not, determine ways that your life could communicate those things to your family, neighbors, co-workers, and anyone who sees you on a regular basis.

3. Daniel's restraint in telling Nebuchadnezzar the bad news about his coming humiliation demonstrated his compassion. When you communicate the message of God's salvation and judgment, do you do so out of love or out of bitterness toward one who is indifferent to the gospel you preach? Read 2 Timothy 2:24-26. What qualities should you demonstrate as you share the good news with those who oppose God?

4. God demonstrated His patience in giving Nebuchadnezzar twelve months to repent. But Nebuchadnezzar had little regard for the kindness and patience of God that should have led him to repentance (Rom. 2:4). Having experienced God's kindness and patience yourself, do you show those qualities toward others who have failed to respond to you in an appropriate way? If not, determine to be patient and kind to those in your life toward whom it is toughest to be that way. Think back on the kindness and patience of God that led you to repentance, and thank Him for His example.

6
Divine Graffiti: The End of an Empire

Outline

Introduction

Lesson
I. The Account
   A. The Scene (vv. 1-4)
      1. The background of Belshazzar (v. 1*a*)
         a) The chronology of the predecessors
            (1) Nebuchadnezzar
            (2) Amel-marduk
            (3) Neriglissar
            (4) Labashi-marduk
            (5) Nabonidus
         b) The conquest by the Persians
      2. The banquet of Belshazzar (vv. 1*b*-4)
         a) Implied indifference (vv. 1*b*-2)
         b) Idolatrous immorality (vv. 3-4)
   B. The Sign (vv. 5-6)
      1. The hand (v. 5)
      2. The horror (v. 6)
         a) Haggai 2:7
         b) Zephaniah 1:15-18
   C. The Shortcoming (vv. 7-9)
      1. The request (v. 7*a*)
      2. The reward (v. 7*b*)
      3. The reading (v. 8)
      4. The result (v. 9)
   D. The Summons (vv. 10-16)
      1. The queen's recollection (vv. 10-11*a*)
      2. Daniel's reputation (vv. 11*b*-12)

87

Introduction

Daniel 5 details the end of the great Babylonian Empire. By the close of the chapter, we will see the transition described in Nebuchadnezzar's image from the head of gold (the Babylonian Empire) to the chest and arms of silver (the Medo-Persian Empire).

Ezekiel 18:20 could well be the theme of Daniel 5: "The soul that sinneth, it shall die." Daniel 5 is a vivid commentary on the fact that sin results in death, not only in the life of an individual, but also in the life of a nation or empire. The Babylonian Empire was once the glorious head of gold—the crown of the times of the Gentiles. But gradually it deteriorated into debauchery until the hour of its eventual doom. The Medo-Persian army then put an end to a great and historic era.

Daniel 5 gives us insight into how a kingdom as wealthy, vast, and powerful as the Babylonian Empire could fall. The first scene we will look at is set during a raucous feast. In the midst of it God pronounced doom on the empire, and after a few hours that destruction came. I believe all civilizations follow this pattern: they rise to great heights, become filled with pride, are characterized by self-indulgence and materialism, and then begin to descend into debauchery until they are destroyed. Psalm 9:17 says, "The wicked shall be turned into sheol, and all the nations that forget God." When a nation forgets God, its doom is certain.

First we will examine the historical account of the fall of the Babylonian Empire, and then we will make some important applications.

Lesson

I. THE ACCOUNT

A. The Scene (vv. 1-4)

1. The background of Belshazzar (v. 1a)

"Belshazzar, the king."

For years critics have said that the book of Daniel is inaccurate because they believed that Belshazzar never existed—that there was no historical record of such a man. However, when archaeologists discovered what is called "The Nabonidus Cylinder," history acquired its first known record of Belshazzar. Approximately thirty-six years old at the time of Daniel 5, Belshazzar was decadent, dissolute, idolatrous, immoral, impious, and unworthy to rule. Although he was co-regent with his father, Nabonidus, Belshazzar was sitting in the seat of royalty the night Babylon fell.

a) The chronology of the predecessors

(1) Nebuchadnezzar (c. 605-562 B.C.)

Seventy years had passed since Daniel and his friends were taken captive (Dan. 1). By this time Daniel was in his eighties. About twenty-three years had passed since Nebuchadnezzar's humiliation and recognition of the true God (Dan. 4). After a reign of forty-three years (during seven of which he was insane), Nebuchadnezzar died in 562 B.C. Although Daniel doesn't record anything between the reigns of Nebuchadnezzar and Belshazzar, extrabiblical history, combined with other biblical references, fills the gap. After Nebuchadnezzar died, the empire began to decline. He was followed by his son.

(2) Amel-marduk (c. 562-559 B.C.)

The Bible refers to that son as Evil-merodach in 2 Kings 25:27-30 and Jeremiah 52:31-34. He released Jehoiakim, the king of Judah, from prison and put him in a privileged position in the Babylonian court. Amel-marduk reigned for only two years before he was assassinated by his brother-in-law Neriglissar.

(3) Neriglissar (c. 559-555 B.C.)

Jeremiah 39:3, 13 refers to Neriglissar as Nergal-sharezer. He was an official under Nebuchadnezzar who apparently was involved in helping release Jeremiah from prison. Neriglissar reigned four years before his own death. He was succeeded by his son, Labashi-marduk.

(4) Labashi-marduk (c. 555 B.C.)

Labashi-marduk, a child regent, reigned only
nine months. He was beaten to death by conspir-
ators, who appointed a successor, Nabonidus.

(5) Nabonidus (c. 555-539 B.C.)

Nabonidus reigned sixteen years until he was defeated by Cyrus, the Medo-Persian emperor. Although Nabonidus was appointed as monarch,
he was not related to Nebuchadnezzar, so he
didn't have a right to the throne. Apparently that
fact intimidated him, for he sought to secure his
claim by marrying into the royal family (through
either a widow or a daughter of Nebuchadnezzar). This woman had a son named Belshazzar.

Maintaining a separate residence at Tema in Ara-
bia, Nabonidus didn't set foot in the city of Babylon for thirteen of the sixteen years he reigned. To
maintain his power in Babylon, he appointed Belshazzar as his co-regent in 552 B.C.

Nabonidus was probably the most capable ruler
to follow Nebuchadnezzar, and he was a very religious man. He excavated former temple sites
and reinstituted abandoned religious rites. He
came from priestly lineage. And he appears to
have been a man of peace and conviction.

b) The conquest by the Persians

Cyrus, the king of the Medes and Persians, soon at-
tacked the Babylonian Empire. He and his army met
Nabonidus and his forces outside the city of Babylon
and defeated them. Nabonidus fled to Borsippa, a
city near Babylon, where he was eventually taken
captive. He was then exiled to Carmania, a province
near Persia, where he died. He never saw Babylon
again.

When Daniel 5 begins, Nabonidus has already been defeated, and the Medes and Persians have held the city of Babylon under siege for several months.

2. The banquet of Belshazzar (vv. 1b-4)

    a) Implied indifference (vv. 1b-2)

    "Belshazzar, the king, made a great feast to a thousand of his lords, and drank wine before the thousand. Belshazzar, while he tasted the wine, commanded to bring the golden and silver vessels which his father, Nebuchadnezzar, had taken out of the temple which was in Jerusalem, that the king, and his princes, his wives, and his concubines, might drink from them."

    It might seem hard to understand how Belshazzar could host a party while the city was surrounded by Medo-Persians, but not when you consider how formidable Babylon was. The city was almost fifteen miles square, according to Herodotus, and had walls that were at least 80 feet thick and 350 feet high with one hundred massive bronze gates in them (*The Histories* 1:181). The Babylonians also had an abundance of water, for the Euphrates River flowed through the middle of the city.

    Seated on a raised platform, Belshazzar began drinking before the thousand lords that had gathered for the huge feast. That he tasted wine (v. 2) implies he became drunk. He then called for the gold and silver vessels. When Nebuchadnezzar, his relative, first took captives from Jerusalem, he desecrated the Temple and took all the gold and silver vessels used by the priests. He had them stored in his own temple in Babylon to prove that his gods were more powerful than the God of Israel. Apparently those vessels had remained undisturbed until Belshazzar, in the midst of his drunken stupor, determined to mock the God of Israel. So he commanded that all the vessels which represented Him be used as utensils from which to drink. That was an act of desecration and blasphemy.

92

Belshazzar wasn't totally uninformed about the God of Israel; he knew that He had made Nebuchadnezzar a raving maniac for seven years. The fact that he knew God had revealed dreams and visions through Daniel is revealed in his later conversation with Daniel. But in the midst of his folly, he mocked God, aware that such an act was blasphemous. He challenged God—and God accepted the challenge.

b) Idolatrous immorality (vv. 3-4)

"They brought the golden vessels that were taken out of the temple of the house of God, which was at Jerusalem; and the king, and his princes, his wives, and his concubines, drank from them. They drank wine, and praised the gods of gold, and of silver, of bronze, of iron, of wood, and of stone."

The descending value of precious gold to worthless stone indicates that Belshazzar and his guests praised their deities. They used the utensils set apart for the true God to worship their false gods. It was a wicked scene.

B. The Sign (vv. 5-6)

1. The hand (v. 5)

"In the same hour came forth fingers of a man's hand, and wrote over against the lampstand upon the plaster of the wall of the king's palace; and the king saw the part of the hand that wrote."

In the midst of the revelry, a supernatural hand appeared from God. God's patience had come to an end, just as it had with those on the earth at the time of the Flood, when He said, "My Spirit shall not always strive with man" (Gen. 6:3). When the people at the feast saw the hand, immediately the drinking and singing stopped. Deathly silence and fear fell over them. The fingers of the hand began to write on a wall that was illuminated by a lampstand. Since the brightest lighting was usually placed where the king sat, it is likely that

93

the fingers wrote on the plaster wall directly above his head.

Archaeologist Robert Koldewey, during his excavation of the palace of Babylon from the time of Belshazzar, found a large room, 55 feet wide and 169 feet long with plaster walls—a significant detail that fits with the biblical record. At the end of the room was a niche in the wall where he believed the king sat so that he would be elevated before the people (*The Excavations at Babylon* [London: MacMillan, 1914], pp. 88-89, 103-4).

2. The horror (v. 6)

"Then the king's countenance was changed, and his thoughts troubled him, so that the joints of his loins were loosed, and his knees smote one against another."

Suddenly a face probably flushed red by wine turned ashen. Although Belshazzar didn't appear to be troubled by a natural foe outside his gate, he was greatly troubled by a supernatural foe inside the palace. Sheer terror gripped his heart. The joints of his hips weakened, which means that all his strength left him. He couldn't stand because of his shaking knees (cf. Nah. 2:10). Such fear will again manifest itself in the future.

a) Haggai 2:7—"I will shake all nations, and the desire of all nations shall come." God shook one nation near the beginning of the times of the Gentiles, and someday He will shake the rest of the nations.

b) Zephaniah 1:15-18—Someday the judgment of God will come upon this world. Zephaniah described it as "a day of wrath, a day of trouble and distress, a day of waste and desolation, a day of darkness and gloominess, a day of clouds and thick darkness, a day of the trumpet and alarm against the fortified cities, and against the high towers. And I will bring distress upon men, that they shall walk like blind men, because they have sinned against the Lord; and their blood shall be poured out like dust, and their flesh like the dung. Neither their silver nor their gold shall be able to deliver them in the day of the Lord's wrath, but the whole land shall be devoured by the fire of his jealousy; for he shall make even a speedy riddance of all those who dwell in the land." That will occur on the day Christ returns.

C. The Shortcoming (vv. 7-9)

1. The request (v. 7a)

"The king cried aloud to bring in the astrologers, the Chaldeans, and the soothsayers."

The same kind of adviser was available to Belshazzar as had been available to Nebuchadnezzar. Such advisers had proved themselves to be useless the first two times they had been called upon (Dan. 2, 4). But Belshazzar was in desperate need of help.

2. The reward (v. 7b)

"The king spoke, and said to the wise men of Babylon, Whosoever shall read this writing, and show me its interpretation, shall be clothed with scarlet, and have a chain of gold about his neck, and shall be the third ruler in the kingdom."

Belshazzar offered a reward to whomever could interpret the writing: a promotion to third ruler of Babylon (Nabonidus being the first and Belshazzar the second). Accompanying the promotion would be a purple robe (representing royalty) and a gold chain (representing highest honor).

3. The reading (v. 8)

"Then came in all the king's wise men; but they could not read the writing, nor make known to the king the interpretation of it."

The wise men couldn't read the writing. Some have suggested that God used an unusual shape for the letters so that only Daniel could read them. Others think the traumatic experience had blinded the reasoning power of the wise men. Perhaps they were so drunk they couldn't read them. We can't be certain.

4. The result (v. 9)

"Then was King Belshazzar greatly troubled, and his countenance was changed in him, and his lords were perplexed."

Apparently Belshazzar had gained some relief, assuming that the wise men would solve the mystery. But when they couldn't, he turned white again. The repeated failure of the wise men to find answers in the midst of a crisis again demonstrates the foolishness of the world's wisdom. First Corinthians 2:14 explains why: "the natural man receiveth not the things of the Spirit of God." God is the Sovereign who rules history. Anyone with a humanistic perspective will never comprehend His plan.

D. The Summons (vv. 10-16)

The dowager queen then entered the room in the confusion of the moment. Most scholars believe she was the mother of Belshazzar since the text says that his wives were already present at the feast (v. 2). In addition, no wife of a king would dare to have entered and addressed the king with such authority as she did.

1. The queen's recollection (vv. 10-11a)

"Now the queen, by reason of the words of the king and his lords, came into the banquet house; and the queen spoke and said, O king, live forever; let not thy thoughts trouble thee, nor let thy countenance be changed. There is a man in thy kingdom, in whom is the spirit of the holy [God]."

Nebuchadnezzar used that last phrase "in whom is the spirit of the holy [God]" thirty years previous (Dan. 4:8-9, 18). As the widow or daughter of Nebuchadnezzar, she probably remembered when he had said that about Daniel.

96

2. Daniel's reputation (vv. 11b-12)

"In the days of thy father light [enlightenment] and understanding [insight] and wisdom [application of knowledge], like the wisdom of the gods, was found in him, whom the king, Nebuchadnezzar, thy father, the king, I say, thy father, made master of the magicians, astrologers, Chaldeans, and soothsayers, forasmuch as an excellent spirit, and knowledge, and understanding, interpreting of dreams, and revealing of hard sentences [riddles], and dissolving of doubts, were found in the same Daniel, whom the king named Belteshazzar. Now let Daniel be called, and he will show the interpretation."

The queen used every noun and adjective she could think of to tell Belshazzar that Daniel was the most intelligent, gifted, and capable man in the realm. Since Daniel could reveal dreams and riddles, she suggested that he be summoned.

3. Daniel's readiness (vv. 13a)

"Then was Daniel brought in before the king."

Daniel wasn't to be found with the other wise men. He had stood alone when he was a teenager. He stood alone when he was a mature man. Now that he was in his eighties he continued to stand alone, refusing to compromise his convictions.

4. The king's request (vv. 13b-16)

a) A verification of Daniel's identity (vv. 13b-14)

"The king spoke and said unto Daniel, Art thou that Daniel, who art of the children of the captivity of Judah, whom the king, my father, brought out of Jewry? I have even heard of thee, that the spirit of [God] is in thee, and that light and understanding and excellent wisdom are found in thee."

Belshazzar had heard about Daniel. But after Nebuchadnezzar died, Daniel apparently had faded into

97

the background, since Belshazzar had to verify his identity. Although Daniel had the rank of a prime minister, Belshazzar obviously hadn't paid much attention to him.

b) An appeal for Daniel's help (vv. 15-16)

"The wise men, the astrologers, have been brought in before me, that they should read this writing, and make known unto me the interpretation of it; but they could not show the interpretation of the thing. And I have heard of thee, that thou canst make interpretations, and dissolve doubts; now, if thou canst read the writing, and make known to me the interpretation of it, thou shalt be clothed with scarlet, and have a chain of gold about thy neck, and shalt be the third ruler in the kingdom."

Daniel was not impressed by the attention now given him, nor was he interested in being a third ruler in the kingdom. Who would want to be the third ruler in a kingdom that had only a few hours remaining in its history? Daniel wasn't intimidated by monarchs when he was a teenager, and he wasn't about to be intimidated as a man in his eighties.

E. The Sermon (vv. 17-24)

1. The integrity of Daniel (v. 17*a*)

"Daniel answered and said unto the king, Let thy gifts be to thyself, and give thy rewards to another."

Daniel didn't want the king's gifts—they meant nothing to him. Daniel had great character and courage. We need more men like him in our day. So many people strive to be rich, powerful, and famous. But Daniel wasn't like that—he was filled with holy zeal and had no interest in gifts or rewards. He couldn't be bought because he had integrity.

2. The illustration of Nebuchadnezzar (vv. 17b-21)

"Yet I will read the writing unto the king, and make known to him the interpretation. O thou king, the Most High God gave Nebuchadnezzar, thy father, a kingdom, and majesty, and glory, and honor; and for the majesty that he gave him, all people, nations, and languages trembled and feared before him. Whom he would he slew; and whom he would he kept alive; and whom he would he set up; and whom he would he put down. But when his heart was lifted up, and his mind hardened in pride, he was deposed from his kingly throne, and they took his glory from him. And he was driven from the sons of men, and his heart was made like the beasts, and his dwelling was with the wild asses; they fed him with grass like oxen, and his body was wet with the dew of heaven, till he knew that the Most High God ruled in the kingdom of men, and that he appointeth over it whomsoever he will."

Nebuchadnezzar needed to learn who was sovereign, so God humbled him. Nebuchadnezzar used his God-given authority to pervert justice. He became proud of his power, so God struck him down. For seven years Nebuchadnezzar imagined he was an animal and consequently acted like one. After that divine punishment, he learned that God rules over the kingdoms of men and gives them to whom He chooses.

3. The indictment against Belshazzar (vv. 22-23)

a) He sinned against knowledge (v. 22)

"Thou, his son, O Belshazzar, hast not humbled thine heart, though thou knewest all this."

Belshazzar couldn't claim he was an ignorant pagan. Daniel told him, in effect, that he had sinned against light. Belshazzar knew what had happened to Nebuchadnezzar and that Nebuchadnezzar had eventually attributed to God all that had happened to him. Belshazzar knew that God was responsible for breaking

Nebuchadnezzar's pride. Against that knowledge he sinned and failed to humble his heart.

Such a serious sin provokes the same indictment from God today. He condemns anyone who understands the gospel of Jesus Christ yet refuses to believe in Him.

(1) Hebrews 10:29—"Of how much sorer punishment, suppose ye, shall he be thought worthy, who hath trodden under foot the Son of God, and hath counted the blood of the covenant . . . an unholy thing." There will be greater punishment for someone who knows the truth yet treats it with indifference. Such a person has sinned against light.

(2) Matthew 11:20-24—Christ pronounced horrible judgment on cities in Galilee for their failure to repent in spite of the miraculous works He had done there. He told them that their judgment would be worse than Sodom's because they refused to heed the words and works He said and did in their midst.

b) He blasphemed God (v. 23a)

"But hast lifted up thyself against the Lord of heaven; and they have brought the vessels of his house before thee, and thou, and thy lords, thy wives, and thy concubines, have drunk wine from them."

Belshazzar not only sinned against light and rejected God, but also committed willful blasphemy by desecrating the holy vessels from the Temple in Jerusalem.

c) He committed idolatry (v. 23b)

"Thou hast praised the gods of silver, and gold, of bronze, iron, wood, and stone, which see not, nor hear, nor know; and the God, in whose hand thy breath is, and whose are all thy ways, hast thou not glorified."

100

Belshazzar's sin against knowledge and sins of blasphemy and idolatry constitute a progression: first he knew the truth and turned from it. Then he blasphemed the true God. Finally he worshiped false gods.

4. The intention of God (v. 24)

"Then was the part of the hand sent from him, and this writing was written."

When God saw Belshazzar's sin against light, his blasphemy, and his idolatry, He sent the fingers to write on the wall.

F. The Solution (vv. 25-28)

1. Consummation (vv. 25-26)

"This is the writing that was written, MENE, MENE, TEKEL, UPHARSIN. This is the interpretation of the thing: MENE; God hath numbered thy kingdom, and finished it."

"MENE" means "numbered," or in the vernacular, "Your number is up!" Daniel told Belshazzar that God, who numbers all kingdoms, said his was finished. To make sure Belshazzar understood, God said it twice.

2. Calculation (v. 27)

"TEKEL; Thou art weighed in the balances, and art found wanting."

"TEKEL" has a double meaning: "to be weighed" and "to be found too light." In those days, people would weigh things by putting a standard of weight on one side of the scale and the commodity to be weighed on the other. In effect Daniel told Belshazzar that he had been weighed by God's standard and had come up short. He was too light in his moral value and spiritual virtue.

3. Conquest (v. 28)

"PERES [UPHARSIN], Thy kingdom is divided, and given to the Medes and Persians."

By dropping the first letter of "UPHARSIN," which means "and," along with the "in" at the end, which indicates plurality, we are left with the same consonants Daniel used in verse 28. The root word means "to divide" or "break," indicating that the Babylonian Empire would be broken, or conquered, and taken over by the Medes and Persians.

The literal translation of God's message is this: "Numbered, numbered, too light, divided." It was God's prophecy that Belshazzar's kingdom would be destroyed because it was lacking in moral and spiritual value—it did not meet God's standard. The Medes and the Persians would absorb it into their larger dominion. I'm sure that when Daniel concluded his interpretation for Belshazzar the hall rang with his words.

G. The Sequel (vv. 29-31)

"Then commanded Belshazzar, and they clothed Daniel with scarlet, and put a chain of gold about his neck, and made a proclamation concerning him, that he should be the third ruler in the kingdom. In that night was Belshazzar, the king of the Chaldeans, slain. And Darius, the Mede, took the kingdom, being about threescore and two years old."

The very night of Belshazzar's feast, the Medes and the Persians were just outside the city. It was a night marked for history: the 16th day of Tishri, 539 B.C., corresponding to the 11th or 12th of October. Herodotus tells us that the Medes and the Persians had built a dam on the Euphrates, thereby diverting its flow away from under the wall of the city and into nearby swamp land. When the water level began to fall to knee or waist height, the Medo-Persians marched underneath the wall on the shallow river bed, taking the city by surprise and without a battle (*The Histories*

1:190-91). The great Babylonian Empire fell, and its end was sudden.

II. THE APPLICATION

Babylon fell in 539 B.C. Someday the Babylon of Revelation 17-18, the final world system of the Antichrist, will experience a far greater fall than its predecessor. But between the two, nations throughout history fall for the same reasons. What were the devastating sins that caused Babylon to fall? Some of them are paralleled in America today.

A. Drunkenness (vv. 1-4)

The fall of Babylon occurred when its leaders were drunk. Cyrus was able to capture most of the surrounding cities of Babylon, but Babylon itself resisted all attacks—it appeared to be unassailable. In their drunken debauchery, the Babylonians thought themselves impregnable. Coincidentally, in the same palace two hundred years later, Alexander the Great, though undefeated by all the armies of the world, died of a fever after drinking himself into a stupor (Arrian, *The Campaigns of Alexander* 7:24-26). He repeated Belshazzar's folly.

Alcohol has destroyed many rulers, and it destroys people throughout America. Statistics indicate that there are millions of alcoholics in this country (for specific statistics see Dr. S. I. McMillen's *None of These Diseases* [Old Tappan, N.J.: Revell, 1984], pp. 22-28, 150-51).

B. Pleasure Madness (vv. 1-4)

The Babylonians were having a party while the end of their kingdom was only a few hours away. They didn't understand the seriousness of their situation because they were preoccupied with pleasure: entertainment, illicit sex, dancing, drinking, and feasting. America is in a similar condition. Our nation is preoccupied with sports, movies, TV, sex, and eating out, to name a few of our indulgences. We spend billions of dollars to satisfy our fleshly desires. The entire country is drowning in pleasure madness, unwilling to face the reality that we are on the brink of doom.

C. Immorality (vv. 2-3)

The worship of pagan gods often involved sexual perversion. In digs around Babylon, archaeologists have discovered artifacts engraved with pornographic pictures. But I don't know that their pornography could be any worse than what has appeared in America. Our nation has abandoned itself to vice and lust. When my daughter Melinda was little, she once asked me why three X's were on the marquee of a theater. The little X's at the bottom of her letters carried a completely different meaning.

D. Idolatry (vv. 4, 23)

Babylonian society was destroyed, in part, because of its idolatry. They worshiped man-made gods, having blatantly rejected the true God. Thousands of deities cluttered their culture. Similarly, in our country there are many false messiahs, religious phonies, cults, and occultic practices. And we worship a multitude of secular gods: sex, money, material goods, pleasure, and education, to name a few. We have crowded God out of our country, except for pockets of those who really know Him.

E. Blasphemy (vv. 2-4, 23)

It wasn't enough for Babylon just to reject God; they blasphemed and mocked Him as well. And in America we produce movies that spoof Jesus Christ and make Him into a clown, superstar, or a sinner. We mock God with our empty prayers before congressional meetings and football games. We mock God with religious charlatans who use His holy name to get rich and fill the needs of their egos.

F. Willful Rejection (vv. 18-22)

No nation I know of in the history of the church has had a greater opportunity to hear the gospel than the United States. Yet the majority isn't interested. In Daniel 5:18-22 Daniel reminded Belshazzar of how God revealed Himself to Nebuchadnezzar, yet Belshazzar had willingly sinned against that knowledge. James 4:17 says, "To him that knoweth to do good, and doeth it not, to him it is sin." Many churches throughout this country are either empty

104

or are led by ministers who deny the Word of God. Many turn their backs and willfully reject what they know to be true. Apparently we have learned little from history.

G. Unrelieved Guilt (vv. 6, 9)

Babylonian society was filled with guilt because sin brings guilt. When Belshazzar saw the writing on the wall, his "countenance was changed, and his thoughts troubled him, so that the joints of his loins were loosed, and his knees smote one against another" (v. 6). Belshazzar's guilt convicted him. People interpret what happens to them in light of their conscience, and our consciences can make cowards of us all. After Adam and Eve sinned, God called for Adam (Gen. 3:8). Normally Adam would have responded to God, but instead he hid himself—his conscience convicted him. America is guilt-ridden: never have there been so many psychiatrists, psychologists, and counselors trying help patients deal with problems such as mental illness, alcohol, drugs, misery, and sorrow.

H. Greed and Impure Motives (vv. 7, 16-17)

In Daniel 5:7 Belshazzar promised that whoever interpreted the writing would "be clothed with scarlet, and have a chain of gold about his neck, and . . . be the third ruler in the kingdom." In verses 16-17 he specifically promised that reward to Daniel, although Daniel had no desire for it.

American society, like Babylonian society, is characterized by greed, selfish motives, and a lack of integrity. People bribe policymakers to get what they want. Most people aren't motivated to speak the truth for its own sake; they expect compensation first.

I.   Materialism (vv. 7, 16-17)

In Babylon, power and prestige were equated with the quality of one's clothes and the riches one possessed. Yet I don't think any country has ever experienced wealth for such a long period as has America. There are richer people in the Arab states, but the masses there don't experi-

105

ence what we do here. By world standards the average American is wealthy and decadent.

J. Overconfidence (vv. 1-4, 30-31)

The Babylonians feasted because they thought their city was impregnable. And many believe America is impregnable. But one day an enemy will overtake us easily because we will be so corrupt internally that we won't be able to put up a fight. When Babylon fell, it was reported that not even a spear was thrown. Although Belshazzar and a few others were executed, no battle occurred because the invasion happened so fast. The people believed their resources were enough to protect them.

Such blind confidence is a product of humanism. The Babylonians had forgotten that God rules the kingdoms of men. They exalted themselves as opposed to the Lord of heaven. Similarly, we live in a humanistic day. Man claims to be the master of his fate and the captain of his soul, as W. E. Henley put it in his poem "Invictus," which means "Unconquered." But it is great foolishness to think we have in ourselves all the resources to meet our needs.

K. Corrupt Leadership (vv. 1-4)

All the princes were as drunk as the king and had participated in the same immorality. The soothsayers, Chaldeans, and magicians couldn't offer Belshazzar any answers because they were totally inept. Daniel 5 is a picture of godless leaders filled with guilt, lust, folly, and alcohol. Sad to say, some American leaders are characterized by such vices.

L. The Decline of the Family (vv. 18-22)

It has been observed that Belshazzar wasn't as good as his father, Nabonidus, or his grandfather, Nebuchadnezzar. I think Nebuchadnezzar became a believer, but there was a wide gulf between him and Belshazzar. To me that illustrates the decline of the family, a trend many have observed in America.

M. Pride (v. 22)

Pride was ultimately the cause of Babylon's fall; for Daniel said, "Thou . . . O Belshazzar, hast not humbled thine heart."

Conclusion

A poem magnificently summarizes Daniel 5 and focuses our attention on the condemnation belonging to all who have not received Jesus Christ as Lord and Savior:

> At the feast of Belshazzar and a thousand of his lords,
> While they drank from golden vessels, as the Book of Truth records,
> In the night as they revelled in the royal palace hall,
> They were seized with consternation at the hand upon the wall.
>
> See the brave captive Daniel as he stood before the throng,
> And rebuked the haughty monarch for his mighty deeds of wrong;
> As he read out the writing, 'Twas the doom of one and all,
> For the kingdom was now finished said the hand upon the wall.
>
> See the faith, zeal and courage that would dare to do the right,
> Which the spirit gave to Daniel this the secret of his might.
> In his home in Judea, a captive in its hall,
> He still understood the writing of his God upon the wall.

So our deeds are recorded; there is a hand that's
  writing now.
Sinner, give your heart to Jesus, to His royal man-
  date bow;
For the day is approaching, it must come to one
  and all,
When the sinner's condemnation will be written
  on the wall.

Sin brings destruction. The world's doom is inevitable as things
continue to grow worse. But the Bible promises that those who put
their faith in Jesus Christ will escape the wrath to come (1 Thess.
1:10) and be delivered from the hour of tribulation (Rev. 3:10).
Search your heart and determine if you truly know Christ. We
must first come to Christ and then stand for His truth so that others
may come to know Him as well. God is not willing that any should
perish (2 Pet. 3:9).

Focusing on the Facts

1. According to Ezekiel 18:20, what is the ultimate result of sin
   (see p. 89)?
2. According to Psalm 9:17, when is the doom of a nation certain
   (see p. 89)?
3. What did critics once believe about Belshazzar? Why (see p.
   89)?
4. How much of a time gap exists between Daniel 4 and 5 (see p.
   90)?
5. What happened to the Babylonian Empire after Nebuchadnezzar died (see p. 90)?
6. Why didn't Nabonidus have a right to the throne? How did he
   secure his claim (see p. 91)?
7. How can Nabonidus be considered the most capable ruler to
   follow Nebuchadnezzar (see p. 91)?
8. Why did Belshazzar host a banquet even though he knew that
   Babylon was surrounded by Cyrus's army (see p. 92)?
9. What had Nebuchadnezzar done to show the people that his
   gods were more powerful than the God of Israel? How did Belshazzar mock God (see pp. 92-93)?
10. What did the sudden appearance of the supernatural hand
    communicate about God's patience (see p. 93)?

11. What was Belshazzar's reaction to the hand? When will that same demonstration of fear occur in the future (see p. 94)?

12. What is demonstrated by the wise men's failure to interpret the writing on the wall (see p. 96)?

13. Why had Daniel been remembered by the queen? What did she emphasize (see pp. 96-97)?

14. How did Daniel demonstrate his continuing refusal to compromise his convictions (see p. 97)?

15. Why did Belshazzar have to verify Daniel's identity (see pp. 97-98)?

16. What was Daniel's response to the promised rewards? Why (see p. 98)?

17. What were the three indictments against Belshazzar (see pp. 99-100)?

18. Explain how people can sin against knowledge (see p. 100).

19. Explain the interpretation of the writing on the wall (see pp. 101-102).

20. When was the prophecy fulfilled? How (see p. 102)?

21. In what condition were Babylon's leaders when the city fell (see p. 103)?

22. What distracted the Babylonians from realizing the seriousness of their situation (see p. 103)?

23. What nation has probably had the greatest opportunity to hear the gospel? How has it turned its back on the truth (see p. 104)?

24. Why were the Babylonians so confident? Why was their confidence misplaced (see p. 106)?

25. What was ultimately responsible for the fall of Babylon (see p. 107)?

26. Although sin always has consequences, there is hope in Christ. What does the Bible promise for those who put their faith in Jesus Christ (see p. 108)

Pondering the Principles

1. Rather than trusting in the God Nebuchadnezzar acknowledged as supreme, Belshazzar trusted in the walls and moat around Babylon for his protection. What fortresses do you trust in: modern technology, arms limitation agreements, your salary, friends? Although we need those things, have they, or any others, become a source of confidence that isolates you from trusting God? According to Isaiah 31:1 and 42:17, what had Israel

trusted in other than God? If you believe you need to trust God more, read Psalm 46 and James 4:13-16.

2. When people think of you, what quality do you suppose they remember? Is it holiness, as was true in the case of Daniel? Is there anything preventing you from having a holy reputation? If so, confess it to the Lord and commit yourself to establishing a reputation that will honor God (1 Tim. 3:1-10).

3. When Belshazzar offered a reward, Daniel made clear that he wasn't motivated by what he could gain. How would you have responded? What motivated Daniel to serve the king? Read 1 Thessalonians 2:2-14. How did Paul demonstrate that he had not come to the Thessalonians "with a pretext for greed" (v. 5, NASB)? How did the Thessalonians respond to the message he offered? What example do you see there for you?

4. Belshazzar didn't reflect the morals of his father. That can often happen when parents don't instill in their children the same values they themselves hold. Why did God make such an important issue of the need for the Israelites to be diligent in instructing their children (Deut. 6:6-23)? How effectively did they teach their children (Judg. 2:7-13)? Are you doing everything you can to help insure that your children will not forget the truths you live by? What can you do for and with your children to build their character and their walk with God?

5. Are you seeking to be salt and light (Matt. 5:13-14) in the midst of a dark and decaying world? What are some ways in which you are preserving the world around you from corruption? In what ways are you the light of truth to your relatives, friends, and neighbors? Think of at least two people with whom you need to share the message of salvation, and begin praying for them. Ask God to "open their eyes so that they may turn from darkness to light" (Acts 26:18, NASB).

Scripture Index

Topical Index

Horoscopes. *See* Occultic
practices
Humanism, overconfidence of,
106
Humility
Daniel's. *See* Daniel
See also Pride

Idolatry, 104
Integrity, Daniel's. *See* Daniel
"Invictus," 106
Israel
gentile dominion over. *See*
Eschatology
hope of, 39
See also Jerusalem

Jerusalem
the Babylonian destruction,
54-56
in the days of Abraham, 53
in the days of David, 54
in the days of Jesus, 54
in the days of Joshua, 53
devotion to, 52-53, 66
focal point of, 52-53
future of, 57-58, 61
the Roman destruction, 56-57
the Six-Day War, 57
See also Israel
Judaism
reaching out to Jewish people, 39
See also Israel

Kingdom of God, the
character of, 60-61
consummation of history, 28
establishment of, 58-60
founder of, 61-64
literal nature of, 59-61
See also Eschatology
Koldewey, Robert, excavation
of Babylon, 94

Labashi-marduk, 90-91
Leadership, corrupt, 106
Leupold, H. C.
on Daniel 2:5, 13
on Daniel 2:40, 36
Livingstone, David, his testimo-
ny to Stanley, 76
"Lo! He Comes," 48-49
Lycanthropy, 78-79

Magic. *See* Occultic practices
Malik, Charles, his analysis of
world problems, 42-44,
50
Materialism, 43, 105
McMillen, S. I., on alcoholism,
103
Mechanization. *See* Technology
Medo-Persia, empire of, 33-34,
45
Millennium. *See* Kingdom of
God
Money. *See* Materialism
Movies. *See* Entertainment

Nabonidus, 91-92
Nebuchadnezzar
cynicism of, 12-14
dreams of, 9-21, 28-38, 45-48,
58-65, 74-85
greatness of, 32-33
insanity of, 78-85, 99
pride of, 72-73, 83, 86
religion of, 63-64
repentance of, 73, 84-86
salvation of, 73-74, 84-86
successors of, 90-91
Nergalsharezer. *See* Neriglissar
Neriglissar, 90
Nuclear arms race, 42, 109

Occultic practices
Babylonian, 10-14, 19-20, 75,
95-96

biblical view on, 22-23, 75, 95-96

Oppenheim, A. L., on Chaldean dream reading, 11

Overconfidence, 106, 109

Pleasure. *See* Entertainment
Prayer, Daniel's. *See* Daniel
Premillennialism, 59-60. *See also* Kingdom of God
Pride
    condemnation of, 70-72
    consequences of, 72-73, 107
    See also Daniel, humility of
Progress. *See* Technology
Promotion, God's way of, 65-67

Rejection of God.
    America's. *See* America, unbelief of
    Belshazzar's. *See* Belshazzar, unbelief of
Repentance, Nebuchadnezzar's. *See* Nebuchadnezzar
Roman empire. *See* Rome
Rome
    past empire of, 36-37
    revived empire of, 37-38, 42-48

Sexual immorality, 103-4
Six-Day War. *See* Jerusalem

Sorcery. *See* Occultic practices
Spiritualism. *See* Occultic practices
Sports. *See* Entertainment
Stanley, Henry. *See* Livingstone, David
Success. *See* Promotion

Technology, worship of, 43, 109
Television. *See* Entertainment
Trials, dealing with, 15-16, 21, 23
Trust, in God. *See* God
TV. *See* Entertainment

Unbelief
    America's. *See* America
    Belshazzar's. *See* Belshazzar
United States. *See* America

Voting. *See* Citizenship

Washington, George, on withstanding compromise, 8
Wesley, Charles, the hymn "Lo! He Comes," 48-49
Western alliance, strain in the, 42
Will of God, obeying the, 65-67
Wood, Leon, on Daniel 2:38, 33
Work. *See* Promotion

Moody Press, a ministry of the Moody Bible Institute, is designed for education, evangelization, and edification. If we may assist you in knowing more about Christ and the Christian life, please write us without obligation: Moody Press, c/o MLM, Chicago, Illinois 60610.